TAKE NO THOUGHT

God's Reply to Our Borrowed Anxieties

Dr. Preston R. Winfrey

iUniverse, Inc.
Bloomington

Take No Thought
God's Reply to Our Borrowed Anxieties

iUniverse books may be ordered through booksellers or by contacting:

iUniverse
1663 Liberty Drive
Bloomington, IN 47403
www.iuniverse.com
1-800-Authors (1-800-288-4677)

ISBN: 978-1-4759-9539-8 (sc)
ISBN: 978-1-4759-9540-4 (hc)
ISBN: 978-1-4759-9541-1 (ebk)

Library of Congress Control Number: 2013911122

Printed in the United States of America

iUniverse rev. date: 07/03/2013

DISCLAIMER

CONTENTS

PREFACE

"Take no thought" is a simple, yet powerful statement, made by our Lord. Jesus spoke these words to his followers in an effort to get them to aim higher. Their aim was too low. They were stuck in the pits of worry, anxiety, despair, and doubt and needed a breakthrough. Jesus informed them that they did not need to get bent out of shape worrying about something over which they had no control.

To those today who seek to wrap themselves with blankets of security—food, clothing, shelter, and bank accounts—Jesus offers the same words to us that he offered to our ancestors yesterday: "Take no thought." In other words, do not lose sleep or risk being late for your appointments tomorrow. Should the Lord keep you through the night and allow your eyes to behold a new day, take time to tell him "thanks."

It is my desire to encourage you to take the words of our Christ seriously. I am aware of the disarray, poverty, homelessness, violence, threats of wars and glitches in our world. These thoughts cause deep concern; however, we do have another choice. We can worry, or we can trust the God of the universe to keep his word. He promised never to leave us or forsake us. He sent his only begotten Son into the world to bring us life through his death. Jesus said, "Take no thought." This settles things for me, and I think I'll get some sleep. My God will satisfy all of my needs because this is the kind of God he is. If you trust the Lord, he will satisfy your needs as well.

ACKNOWLEDGMENTS

I must first thank God for his love toward me, shown through his Son, Jesus Christ, who saved me from the darkness that sin caused and brought me into the marvelous light of his Word. I am thankful for the inspiration he gave me to write my thoughts, in an effort to inform and encourage others who, like me, are journeying through this barren land.

Second, I thank God for my parents, Arthur and Nellye Winfrey, for bringing me into the Winfrey family. To my eldest sister, Marcellene, an educator in the Cincinnati School System, I say thanks for encouraging me to write this book while it was fresh in my mind. And along this road of appreciation, I thank Dr. Melvin Banks of Urban Ministries Inc. for his words of wisdom and his counsel when he advised me to expand my views in this book beyond the year 2000.

To all of the other people who are significant in my life and whose encouragement to continue this book has been a great source of inspiration to me, I extend my deep appreciation. This group includes other family members, parishioners from various churches, and a few faithful friends.

Finally, I thank my wife, Dr. Gloria Jene Winfrey, a retired assistant principal and the devoted love of my life, to whom I have had the privilege of being married since Saturday, July 3,

1993, at 6:25 p.m. Thank you for your encouragement, support, patience, and words of affirmation to me about my writing and for editing my work prior to my submission to the publisher. Thank you for believing in me.

PART ONE

Yesterday's Dilemma

"He was a murderer from the beginning, not holding to the truth, for there is no truth in him. When he lies, he speaks his native language, for he is a liar and the father of lies" (John 8:44).

Jesus answered, "It is written: Worship the Lord your God and serve him only.'" (Luke 4:8).

CHAPTER 1

Satan's Lie to Mankind

Now the serpent was more crafty than any of the wild animals the Lord God had made. He said to the woman, "Did God really say, You must not eat from any tree in the garden'?" (Genesis 3:1)

Does the lie Satan fed to Eve when they were in the garden yesterday have any real effect on us today? According to the Word of God, it does. As a matter of fact, all people have been penalized because of man's response to the lie Satan told to the first couple. Eve swallowed this lie yesterday, and that fruit seems to be stuck in our throats today.

I am persuaded that Satan lied to this first human family for several reasons:

- He is "a liar and the father of lies." He can't help himself. He is angry with God and wants to even the score through personal revenge. "You belong to your father, the devil, and you want to carry out your father's desire. He was a murderer from the beginning, not holding to the truth, for there is no truth in him. When he lies, he speaks his native language, for he is a liar and the father of lies" (John 8:44).
- He desires our devotion in an effort to boost his own ego and to insult God: "'You will not certainly die,' the serpent said to the woman. 'For God knows that when

you eat from it your eyes will be opened, and you will be like God, knowing good and evil'" (Genesis 3:4-5).

- He realizes that he is destined for eternal damnation and wants as much company as he can to join him. "And I will put enmity between you and the woman, and between your offspring and hers; he will crush your head, and you will strike his heel" (Genesis 3:15).
- He wants those who are cleansed and saved (by the blood of Jesus) to merely exist without the joy of their salvation. "If we confess our sins, he is faithful and just and will forgive us our sins and purify us from all unrighteousness" (1 John 1:9). "Restore to me the joy of your salvation and grant me a willing spirit, to sustain me" (Psalm 51:12).

<u>The Father of Lies</u>

Lying is one of Satan's attributes. You will find it on his résumé in bold print. Some Jews were misdirected and in great error with respect to Jesus. They bragged about their ties to their ancestor Abraham and boasted about their relationship to God, but were oblivious to the only begotten Son of God. Jesus knew that these Jews were solidly steeped in their traditions, but when it came to the truth concerning the deity of Jesus, there was a loose connection, and the light would not come on for these fellows. Knowing part of the truth is dangerous. Half-truths contain only half the evidence.

How many times have you been in a conversation with another person and said, "Your statement is not true," and he responded, "All I know is what I've said, and that's all I have to say about the matter"? Unfortunately, Satan was using that person as a tool, and he didn't realize it. Satan is empowered when we are in the dark. He knows that where there is no light, darkness will prevail. And where there is darkness, he prevails. "But anyone who hates a brother or sister is in the darkness and walks around in the darkness. They do not know where they are going, because the darkness has blinded them" (1 John 2:11).

I have found that some of the most misinformed people take great delight in, and are successful at, drawing a crowd. Unproven information seems to make headlines in the newspapers. Solomon said, "The tongue of the wise commands knowledge, but the mouth of the fool gushes folly" (Proverbs 15:2). Someone once said, "It is better to remain silent and be thought a fool, than to open your mouth and remove all doubt." I personally have searched for the person who made this statement and was not able to settle on a single person, however, I am persuaded that the genesis of this thought is biblical in nature. Proverbs 17:28 says "Even fools are thought wise if they keep silent, and discerning if they hold their tongues."

The more misinformed a person is, the more opportunities there are for him to voice his opinion. Now, if you think that I am putting down those who are misinformed, I am not. I am stating that to some, ignorance is bliss. Especially in the area of spiritual matters, a lot of ignorance is perpetuated both at and away from the pulpit. You can be saved, sanctified, filled with zeal, and above all most sincere in your efforts to please the Lord, but if you are not aware of Satan and his devices, you will remain ignorant about the devil's strategies.

Satan is a mastermind at seducing people at every level. "How you have fallen from heaven, morning star, son of the dawn! You have been cast down to the earth, you who once laid low the nations!" (Isaiah 14:12).

Satan is not a new kid on the block asking where the candy store is located. He has been around. The Bible reveals that Satan is the deceiver. A deceiver's mission is to introduce his victims to the wrong paths in life. And if you should question his information, he will reason with you until you buy into what he says.

In his book *The Strategies of Satan* (Tyndale House, 1979, pages 16, 19, 25), Warren W. Wiersbe shares three things that Satan does to deceive people.

1. "Satan's Target—Your Mind"
2. "Satan's Weapon—Lies"
3. "Satan's Purpose—To make you ignorant of God's will—Satan attacks God's Word because God's Word reveals God's will."

"Apart from the Word of God, we have no sure understanding of the will of God. The will of God is the expression of love for us."

The Bible is our only defense against the tricks of the devil. The Bible does us good when it is saturated in our hearts. It is never enough just to carry our Bibles around with us, keep them in the packing box when not at the church, and feel mystical because we own them. We need more than a gold cross hanging on a chain around our necks, church membership and a favorite pew, and a good feeling when we hear the top ten gospel songs. We must have the Word of God in our hearts. David said, "I have hidden your word in my heart that I might not sin against you" (Psalm 119:11).

<u>Satan Is Not Threatened</u>

The book of Matthew, chapter 4, describes how Satan boldly approached and challenged Jesus, asking if he were the son of God.

> Then Jesus was led by the Spirit into the wilderness to be tempted by the devil. After fasting forty days and forty nights, he was hungry. The tempter came to him and said, "If you are the Son of God, tell these stones

> to become bread." Jesus answered, "It is written: 'Man shall not live on bread alone, but on every word that comes from the mouth of God." Then the devil took him to the holy city and had him stand on the highest point of the temple. "If you are the Son of God," he said, "throw yourself down. For it is written: "'He will command his angels concerning you, and they will lift you up in their hands, so that you will not strike your foot against a stone." Jesus answered him, "It is also written: 'Do not put the Lord your God to the test.'" Again, the devil took him to a very high mountain and showed him all the kingdoms of the world and their splendor. "All this I will give you," he said, "if you will bow down and worship me." Jesus said to him, "Away from me, Satan! For it is written: 'Worship the Lord your God, and serve him only.'" Then the devil left him, and angels came and attended him. (Matthew 4:1-11)

We must realize that Satan has never been threatened, and never will be threatened, by lukewarm people who rely upon their feelings, emotions, traditions, or old sayings that have been handed down through the years. Satan is not afraid of our church attendance, revival meetings, prayer meetings, or Bible studies, as long as we don't take any of what is real to heart and don't commit to anything: ". . . having a form of godliness but denying its power. Have nothing to do with such people" (2 Timothy 3:5). Satan is not afraid of what people purchase from their church or from the local souvenir shops whose alleged specialty is to get rid of the devil and his demons. People have purchased crosses, light bulbs, candles, powders, statues, and other so-called magical remedies to get rid of a spirit that they cannot see. Even in some churches, the worship leader encourages the congregants to tell Satan to get under their feet (while they stomp him on the head) in order to destroy the devil. I can assure you, Satan loves ignorance, especially when it comes to the people who are saved by grace but are ignorant of the authority of God's Word: "in order that Satan might not outwit us. For we are not unaware of his schemes" (2 Corinthians 2:11).

Satan is not disturbed by the churches that have convinced themselves that there is power in their number, and that they can defeat Satan. Satan loves the Christian who quotes everyone except God. He is not afraid when we shout or run and leap over pews, or of anything else that we enjoy. Just don't grip the truth of God's Word, he says, and all will be well. The Bible instructs us to resist the devil and get closer to God, who is our only protection against Satan. "Submit yourselves, then, to God. Resist the devil, and he will flee from you. Come near to God and he will come near to you. Wash your hands, you sinners, and purify your hearts, you double-minded" (James 4:7-8).

What Threatens Satan?

When you are truly committed to receiving and obeying the Word of God, that will be the dividing line, the place where Satan throws a fit. Satan wants to keep us away from the Bible and its true teachings because he knows that it will lead us to victory. "Jesus answered, 'It is written: Man shall not live on bread alone, but on every word that comes from the mouth of God'" (Matthew 4:4).

When a person commits to the Savior and welcomes the pure Word of God into his heart, his eyes (spiritually) are opened, and he can see clearly. The more clearly a person is able to see, the closer that individual draws to Christ. When you seek to truly please Christ, and do so, you move farther away from Satan. The farther you move away from the devil, the more fiery darts he will throw your way. Satan hates God with a passion:

> How you have fallen from heaven, morning star, son of the dawn! You have been cast down to the earth, you who once laid low the nations! You said in your

> heart, "I will ascend to the heavens; I will raise my throne above the stars of God; I will sit enthroned on the mount of assembly, on the utmost heights of Mount Zaphon. I will ascend above the tops of the clouds; I will make myself like the Most High." But you are brought down to the realm of the dead, to the depths of the pit. (Isaiah 14:12-15)

Satan seeks to interrupt our friendship and fellowship with God and takes every opportunity he gets to bad-mouth God and cast doubt on our path. When Satan saw Eve alone in the garden, he knew that she was innocent and unaware of good and evil, right and wrong. When they met in the garden, Satan introduced Eve to a new, exciting, and exhilarating movement: SIN. Even though she knew the truth, Satan convinced her that she could operate independently of God. He assured her that God had left something out of his plan for her and Adam and that he had just what she needed in order to be whole:

> Now the serpent was more crafty than any of the wild animals the Lord God had made. He said to the woman, "Did God really say, 'You must not eat from any tree in the garden'?" The woman said to the serpent, "We may eat fruit from the trees in the garden, but God did say, 'You must not eat fruit from the tree that is in the middle of the garden, and you must not touch it, or you will die.'" "You will not certainly die," the serpent said to the woman. "For God knows that when you eat from it your eyes will be opened, and you will be like God, knowing good and evil." When the woman saw that the fruit of the tree was good for food and pleasing to the eye, and also desirable for gaining wisdom, she took some and ate it. She also gave some to her husband, who was with her, and he ate it. Then the eyes of both of them were opened, and they realized they were naked; so

> they sewed fig leaves together and made coverings for themselves. (Genesis 3:1-7)

Note Satan's smooth approach to Eve: "Did God really say, 'You must not eat from any tree in the garden'"? The calculating Satan was able to predict her response. His timing was good. His approach was masterful. His camouflage worked. Eve didn't see him for who he was. Satan manipulated Eve to steer her to where he wanted her to go, and she went there. It is important to note that Satan can never make people obey him. They decide to obey him. Satan didn't make Eve eat from the tree of knowledge. He made her hungry. When a person is hungry, he will eat what is available. While Eve had a choice, Satan's menu appeared most appetizing at the time, so she ordered from his menu.

The same is true of us today. If we are hungry enough, we will eat whatever is placed before us, even if a stranger brings it to us. I have seen this principle at work with children who declared that they didn't eat certain foods. They were permitted to go without eating; and then when they became hungry enough, they not only ate what was prepared for them, they asked for seconds. This meal was so good to Eve that she took a "doggie bag" home to her husband Adam. And they both enjoyed the forbidden fruit. "When the woman saw that the fruit of the tree was good for food and pleasing to the eye, and also desirable for gaining wisdom, she took some and ate it. She also gave some to her husband, who was with her, and he ate it" (Genesis 3:6).

According to Genesis 2:16-17 and 3:2-3, this couple clearly knew what they should and should not do. God does not have a speech impediment; the boundary line was clear. And Adam and Eve did not have amnesia. They knew what was expected of them, and they chose to do their own thing. What was their problem? Had God been unfair to them?

And what is our problem? Has God been unfair to us? David said, "I was young and now I am old, yet I have never seen the righteous forsaken or their children begging bread" (Psalm 37:25).

We do not have a single justifiable reason for failing to trust God. God has been good to us. Not to trust God is a matter of personal will. Satan cannot force us to disobey God. We choose either to obey God or not to obey him. The first couple disobeyed God by virtue of their own individual wills, as seen in Genesis 3:6. How far removed are we from Adam and Eve? Do we respond any differently to the directives God gives us? Satan is still lying to us and, somehow, I am convinced that we are trying to find some truth in this devil.

God has given to each of us a will to do as we see best. In light of what we know, do we do right or wrong? We can will to sin and we can choose the sin we wish to commit. The contrast to this issue is, we cannot choose the consequences that follow our sin. We don't know when or where the consequences will strike. Knowing this, let us make good choices for the rest of our lives.

CHAPTER 2

You Know the Truth

> And the Lord God commanded the man, "You are free to eat from any tree in the garden; but you must not eat from the tree of the knowledge of good and evil, for when you eat of it you will surely die." (Genesis 2:16-17)

Is it really true that what you don't know can't hurt you? How many times have you heard that statement? Before you answer this question too hastily, you might need to read between the lines to see the real issue at hand. You should also assess what impact the decision you make will have on your life.

Growing up, I learned several clichés from the community. I was pretty much like other people in this regard. I learned quickly the things not meant for me to learn. My peers, adults, and others all taught me things that veered from the truth as I knew it. Nevertheless, I learned these clichés because I was convinced that I would have an edge on others.

One cliché frequently used was "what I don't know can't hurt me." I took great delight in using this phrase because it allowed me to escape from negative consequences (or so I thought). I used it often at school and at play. My compensation was poor grades, constant trips to the principal's office, and more whippings than I want to remember. I knew better, but this cliché was my disclaimer.

I can remember times when my mother specifically instructed me to do a chore in the house. I purposely failed to do as I had been instructed. In my heart, I wanted to believe that my mother would forget what I had been told to do. I wasted an inordinate amount of time and energy trying to ignore what I knew deep in my heart. Don't ask me why I did this. Perhaps it was just a game that I enjoyed playing with myself and others. At any rate, my mother didn't find the humor in this kind of game. My teachers and the people in the church also let me know that that they did not appreciate my selective memory. What they said to do, they meant. I share this to point out that I knew what was expected of me. I knew the truth. No matter how I tried to convince people that I was misinformed, I knew the truth.

Conflicting Instructions

There were times when I was given clear instructions to do or not to do a certain thing. Then Mr. Neighbor asked me to do just the opposite. Did I know the truth? Yes, I knew the truth, but Mr. Neighbor asked me to do him a favor. Why did I disobey what had been clearly explained to me? I had an incentive. Mr. Neighbor was paying me to run his errand. If I were to get caught, the money would more than compensate for the punishment. But deep in my heart, I believed I would never get caught.

Have there been times in your life when you knew the truth but decided against it, only to reap the consequences of your decision? Perhaps you found yourself in traffic court, standing before the judge with the arresting officer on your left. You plead to the judge that you are innocent, because this was your first time traveling down this particular highway. You didn't know that you had exceeded the speed limit because you were moving with the flow of traffic. The judge says to you, "Ignorance of the law is no excuse."

You are in the unemployment line because you lost your temper in the office, once again. You tried to explain to your supervisor that a coworker made you slap her, but the supervisor didn't buy it. His parting question was, "How did she make you slap her? Did she grab your hand and force you to do it?"

What a person is really saying in these situations is "I'm not responsible for this. Don't mistreat me because I was oblivious to what was going on." A teenage girl tries to reason with her parents that the pregnancy was a mistake caused in part by her young age. The girl argues that her friends told her that nothing would happen the first time. Her father reminds her of their previous conversations regarding self-respect, chastity, and even the dangers of being in the wrong place and compromising your values. No matter how much this daughter insists that "they told me nothing would happen to me," the fact remains—she knew the truth.

In the May/June 1999 issue of *Discipleship Journal*, Lisa Marzano asks "Too Busy to Obey?" She argues that "we get so busy and self absorbed in our hectic world that it is easy to ignore the prompting of the Holy Spirit . . . There's no magic formula for obedience, but there are several things we can do to help us follow him better: Practice listening, be honest, and don't be afraid to be different."

We always want to be like someone or something else we were never intended to be. This is a sin and a shame. Ancient Israel wanted to be like other nations. They wanted an earthly king to rule them. They were not satisfied with the leadership God provided. They wanted something else. We are like this today. We are not content with what we have or who we are. Why must we always have more? What drives us to want what "the Joneses" have? I find it interesting that cost is never a factor whenever we are bent on getting what we want. A person will be behind with their rent and will still splurge on something he wants. This person clearly understands the consequences associated with not paying rent, but will act as though time is on his side. When asked, "What will you do if you have to go to court?" many people have remarked, "I'll cross that bridge when I get to it." This is a sad example of how some people mishandle their business.

Allow me to digress for a moment. As a child in my mother's house, I was once on dish detail. I was to wash dishes and put them away, or else! I opted to play, watch television, and go to sleep. When my mother came home from work at 1:00 a.m. and found the dishes unwashed, she woke me up and made me do what I should have done hours earlier. You see, I knew the truth. I just simply chose not to do what I should have done and did not consider the consequences of my disobedience.

No One Will Escape God

The scriptures tell us no person will ever be able to stand before God and say that he didn't know right from wrong. God has revealed his truth to us and has placed it in our hearts. Writing to Christians in Rome, Paul offered these words:

> The wrath of God is being revealed from heaven against all the godlessness and wickedness of men who suppress the truth by their wickedness, since what may be known about God is plain to them, because God has made it plain to them. For since the creation of the world God's invisible qualities—his eternal power and divine nature—have been clearly seen, being understood from what has been made, so that men are without excuse. For although they knew God, they neither glorified him as God nor gave thanks to him, but their thinking became futile and their foolish hearts were darkened. Although they claimed to be wise, they became fools and exchanged the glory of the immortal God for images made to look like mortal

> man and birds and animals and reptiles. Therefore, God gave them over in the sinful desires of their hearts to sexual impurity for the degrading of their bodies with one another. They exchanged the truth of God for a lie, and worshiped and served created things rather than the Creator—who is forever praised. Amen. (Romans 1:18-25)

God has planted his Word in our hearts, and we are without excuses. Even the issue concerning salvation is a "done deal." No person can ever stand before God and state that he didn't have an opportunity to hear a response to the Gospel. "For the grace of God that brings salvation has appeared to all men. It teaches us to say 'no' to ungodliness and worldly passions, and to live self-controlled, upright and godly lives in this present age" (Titus 2:11-12). "And this gospel of the kingdom will be preached in the whole world as a testimony to all nations, and then the end will come" (Matthew 24:14).

There is no hiding place from God. The chorus of a song titled "No Place, No Where" goes like this: "You might run to the mountains. You might run down to the sea. You go to the rocks, to hide your face, the rocks cry, 'You can't hide in me.'"

The psalmist asked:

> Where can I go from your Spirit? Where can I flee from your presence? If I go up to the heavens, you are there; if I make my bed in the depths, you are there. If I rise on the wings of the dawn, if I settle on the far side of the sea, even there your hand will guide me, your right hand will hold me fast. If I say, "Surely the darkness will hide me and the light become night around me," even the darkness will not be dark to you; the night will shine like the day, for darkness is as light to you. For you created my inmost being; you knit me together in my mother's womb. I praise you because

> I am fearfully and wonderfully made; your works are wonderful, I know that full well. My frame was not hidden from you when I was made in the secret place. When I was woven together in the depths of the earth, your eyes saw my unformed body. All the days ordained for me were written in your book before one of them came to be. (Psalm 139:7-16)

There is no escape from God's truth. Truth will rise. Truth has been thrown into the deepest sea, but it cannot be drowned. No matter what you attach to the other end of it, truth will float to the top in time. Truth cannot be burned. It was cast into the fiery furnace, and it came out of the furnace without even a hint of smoke: ". . . and the satraps, prefects, governors and royal advisers crowded around them. They saw that the fire had not harmed their bodies, nor was a hair of their heads singed; their robes were not scorched, and there was no smell of fire on them" (Daniel 3:27).

A person can pretend that they do not know the truth, but the truth will haunt them until he confesses it. Eve knew the truth. She was not one bit confused. Satan was a smooth operator, and he was persuasive. Using a bit of my imagination, Satan posted a "for sale" sign, and Eve closed the deal. She knew the truth but changed it to suit her own purpose. She wanted to feel justified about her rebellion. Her lust got the best of her.

Note what God told the couple: "But you must not eat from the tree of the knowledge of good and evil, for when you eat of it you will surely die" (Genesis 2:17).

Now compare that to what Eve said to the devil: "But God did say, 'You must not eat fruit from the tree that is in the middle of the garden, and you must not touch it, or you will die'" (Genesis 3:3).

Eve was not slow. The question is, why would a person who clearly knows the voice of God act as though she never heard his voice? What makes people add to and delete from God's Word at will? Do you think they know that the day is coming when they will give an account for their stewardship? Do you think they care? Do you care? Trusting the wrong source can ruin anyone. With all of the competition for our attention in the world today, it is necessary that we know, understand, and properly respond to the voice of authority. Our true source, according to Psalm 24:8, is the Lord. He is "strong and mighty," and he is "mighty in every battle." He is the "king of glory." If a person chooses to listen to the wrong sources, the outcome can be fatal. If a person blows his opportunity to be saved from his sins and dies, he will have the rest of eternity to regret his decision. Revelation 20:15 assures us that there is no second chance to save your soul once physical death has taken place: "Anyone whose name was not found written in the book of life was thrown into the lake of fire."

Who Will You Follow?

From the very beginning of man's creation, he has had the freedom to choose his destiny. Even though he did not know the difference between right and wrong, freedom to choose remained his pleasure. Man made his choice. Evil would be his model. Since that time, both paths have been made clear to all who came after Adam. The issue was and remains, who will you follow? Will it be God or the gods of the earth?

> Moses said, "'. . . Whoever is for the Lord, come to me.' And all the Levites rallied to him." (Exodus 32:26)
>
> Joshua made his choice and said to the people: "But if serving the Lord seems undesirable to you, then choose for yourselves this day whom you will serve, whether the gods your forefathers served beyond the river, or the gods of the Amorites, in whose land you

> are living. But as for me and my household, we will serve the Lord." (Joshua 24:15)

> Elijah said to the prophets of Baal, "'. . . How long will you waver between two opinions? If the Lord is God, follow him; but if Baal is God, follow him.' But the people said nothing." (1 Kings 18:21)

While we are tempted and prone to sin, we can thank God for Jesus, who, as Paul described in his first letter to the church in Corinth, makes a way of escape for us. The Lord has promised to be our sustenance in the time of trouble and temptation. Remember the words of Horatio R. Palmer, who wrote this famous hymn: Yield Not to Temptation

> Yield not to temptation, for yielding is sin;
> Each victory will help you, some other to win.
> Fight manfully onward, dark passions subdue;
> Look ever to Jesus, he'll carry you through.
> Ask the Savior to help you, comfort, strengthen and keep you;
> He is willing to aid you, he will carry you through.

In addition, we should remember that no matter what storms may come our way and rock our little boats, we are never alone. The nineteenth-century hymn writer Ludie Pickett wrote these words: *Never Alone*,

> "The world's fierce winds are blowing—temptation's sharp and keen;
> I have a peace in knowing my Savior stands between;
> He stands to shield me from danger when all my friends are gone—
> He promised never to leave me, never to leave me alone."

This help is available now, and it was available when Eve needed help. Eve's problem was that she didn't ask for the Lord's help. She tried to handle Satan independently of God. She didn't know who she was dealing with. Satan was too strong, clever, sagacious, and too knowledgeable for her to handle. He is the same devil today. We are no match for Satan. This devil is no clown, wearing a painted suit with horns on his head. He is evil personified. He has been around for centuries. He has gone through the world seeking people to sift as wheat. He is still in business today, seeking those he can steal, kill, and destroy.

The truth has already been established. Jesus is the Way, the only way. He is the truth, the only truth. Jesus is the life, the only life. His Word is truth. Do you know him? He is our refuge in the time of storms: "God is our refuge and strength, an ever-present help in trouble" (Psalm 46:1). He is a hiding place when the enemy of our soul comes upon us, to eat up our flesh. "For in the day of trouble he will keep me safe in his dwelling; he will hide me in the shelter of his sacred tent and set me high upon a rock." (Psalm 27:5).

He makes a way for us out of no way. You can't deny this great truth. As our elders used to say, "You know. And if you don't know, you had better act like you know."

According to Romans 14:12, every person will have to answer to God for their stewardship. In other words, whether or not a person is saved, he will have a judgment to attend after his earthly life has concluded. Now if you are saved, you will appear before the Judgment Seat of Christ: "For we must all appear before the judgment seat of Christ, so that each of us may receive what is due us for the things done while in the body, whether good or bad" (2 Corinthians 5:10).

And as for those who never accepted the Lord Jesus Christ into their hearts and trusted him for saving their souls, they will go before the Great White Throne Judgment to be judged and condemned to eternal damnation:

> And I saw the dead, great and small, standing before the throne, and books were opened. Another book was opened, which is the book of life. The dead were judged according to what they had done as recorded in the books. The sea gave up the dead that were in it, and death and Hades gave up the dead that were in them, and each person was judged according to what they had done. Then death and Hades were thrown into the lake of fire. The lake of fire is the second death. Anyone whose name was not found written in the book of life was thrown into the lake of fire. (Revelation 20:12-15)

You may be wondering to yourself, "Now what is this author's point?" I am so glad you asked this question, because my point is this: You can continue acting as though, and giving others the impression that, you don't know the things you know. But rest assured: the day will come when you have to give an account of your stewardship and be compensated for those times you allegedly lost your memory.

CHAPTER 3

Wheeling and Dealing with Satan

> "You will not surely die," the serpent said to the woman. "For God knows that when you eat of it your eyes will be opened, and you will be like God, knowing good and evil." (Genesis 3:4-5)

> Jesus said to him, "Away from me, Satan! For it is written: 'Worship the Lord your God, and serve him only.'" (Matthew 4:10; recommended reading: Matthew 3:13-4:11 because it tells of the deity of Jesus and his commitment to his mission prior to his being led into the wilderness to be tempted by the devil

In the 1960s and 1970s, there was a TV game show titled *Let's Make A Deal.* (this game show is still on the air with Wayne Brady as the host.) The host, Monty Hall, made all sorts of bargains with his audience. Many in the audience traveled from near and far and wore all sorts of costumes. It seemed as if the host asked the people wearing the most interesting costumes to participate. It appeared to me that people were picked at random. In the audience, tons of excitement and energy was generated. People knew they were there in hopes to make a deal and also that they knew if picked, they were taking a chance on the deals they made.

Monty Hall sometimes enticed a guest with an amount of money. Then he would ask if they wanted to trade the money for what was behind a curtain on the stage. By this time, the audience would be screaming and coaching the contestant to "take the curtain, take the curtain." Many times the person making the deal was persuaded to take the curtain, though many remained a bit unsure. The excitement was almost more than the contestant could handle. Hall would say, "You're running out of time, and you must decide." While the excitement level was high and people were shouting, the person finally made a decision and was ready to see what he had won. First, however, the host had another proposition. This time, the stakes were higher. "I'll give you an additional $200 if you refuse to look behind the curtain."

By now the contestant was not only excited, he was anxious and curious. Silently, he seemed to ask himself, *what's behind that curtain that he doesn't want me to get?* He insisted that he wanted the curtain. The host offered to toss in an extra $100 if he'd take the cash instead of the curtain. This proposition brought the total to $500. The contestant made a decision: *I want the curtain!* Hall ordered the curtain opened. The contestant ended up with a pair of sneakers without shoe strings. All of the excitement was gone. He was embarrassed for several reasons. First, he was on national television. Second, he could have had $500, had he left well enough alone. Finally, he did not need a pair of sneakers. He tried to laugh, but what he felt inside his heart showed on his face. The host told him, "You've been a good sport," and prepared for the next deal.

Of course, many people actually made good and rewarding decisions on *Let's Make a Deal*. After all, it was only a game show. The purpose was twofold: having fun for one hour and win money or prizes. I imagine that it must have been fun just to be in the audience and cheer others on. However, I also believe that there were countless participants who were stressed out during and after the show because they couldn't afford to lose.

I find it most interesting that many people love taking unnecessary chances in life. Even when he knows the stakes are high, a person often will dive right in. Most people see the positive side of the game show: that it is safe and will not harm one's life. But let's look at another aspect of this show. This is when a person loses and his countenance is low, the host will sometimes give a consolation gift to the contestant if he didn't handle losing very well.

Life Is Not a Game Show

It's wishful thinking to believe that life should just be like a game show. Game shows start on time, have a few commercials, and end after twenty-two minutes if it is a half hour show. If it is an hour show, you can count on forty-two minutes of game time. However, in life, no one offers you a gift when you lose. Many people believe in luck. I once did. Now I believe luck is for the misinformed. Do you know people who are advocates for luck and taking chances? They seem to have faith that something out of the ordinary will happen; they label that result as luck. Even when the consequences are known to be negative, they go at it full steam ahead.

Often people are seduced by a smooth-talking person or by something that promises to make their lives easier. The seducer or temptation convincingly conveys the message that "you have nothing to lose" and makes you an offer too good to refuse. When telemarketers call us at home, they tell us that they are offering us a great deal. Some will seek to convince you that if you do not accept their offer, you will regret it. As it has been said for many years, "If that sounds too good to be true, it is." Many of the people who accepted those offers from these con artists are now living in the poor house, on the streets homeless, trapped in prostitution, or in jail, mental institutions and some are dead in their graves.

Promises, promises, and more promises. Con artists come a dime-a-dozen. They will wheel and deal with whoever participates in their games.

You find these people in the subways, loaded with gimmicks and tricks. They are masters at deception. They use cards, cups, and anything else to deceive the unaware person. Con artists seem to pop up from nowhere, willing to take you places you have never been. Sometimes they pose as friends who understand what you are going through. Sometimes they introduce you to a pill or a drink that promises to take away your pain. They will even give you a free smoke or sniff, to make sure that you are sincere about having your woes subside. They give you just enough to hook you, and then they reveal that, effective tomorrow, you must pay rent.

Unfortunately, there are con artists in the religious field who "play" innocent people. These con artists assure their victims that the spirit has given them special anointing and revelations, and they promise to give people healing, special blessings, prosperity, peace, the destruction of their enemies, and lives free of trouble. Like those of all other con men, their stories sound legitimate until the lights come on. Then the real deal comes to the surface, and it is usually too late to escape. Once you are trapped, you either must submit to imprisonment or work through the entrapment. We can thank the Lord that his grace has allowed many people to break through the snares of the enemy. Unfortunately, countless victims never find freedom. They lose their families, positions in life, friends and associates, reputations, dignity, and even their lives. What a price to pay for falling victim to a con game. The sad part is that many of these people were not dumb. They just made some bad judgment calls, which cost them dearly. They knew what they were up against, but chose to believe that things would be different for them. Many people say "I can beat the system," but this is only a myth. The system usually beats the person.

Don't Play Yourself

The person who dates and develops an intimate relationship with someone who is married is only wasting his time. You cannot build a solid relationship with someone who is not committed to you. Here are a few reasons why these arrangements don't work:

1. The married person cannot properly function on two separate foundations.
2. You will never have the cheater's full attention or devotion.
3. He or she will have to sneak away from home to spend time with you.
4. The demands for the relationship will be one-sided (all on you).
5. You will get the other person's leftovers, nothing of any real significance.
6. You will still spend most of the important days alone.
7. The relationship will not be the main course, only a desert.
8. You will require more than the married person can deliver.

Then there is Mr. Boo, whose palm is itching, and he feels that there is a winning streak in his system. So off to the races or the casino he goes. "Maybe I'll go to the boat casino where the slot machines are sure to bring me luck." Mr. Boo goes to the casino and uses the rent money because he feels lucky. Only later does he discover that he took his luck to the wrong machine, so he borrows money from someone in an effort to win his money back. Well, you can guess what happens: he loses again. Now he owes his landlord and his neighbor. Mr. Boo can't understand what went wrong. His intuition failed him, but he'll try again. This time he borrows from a friend who is not aware of his new addiction. Mr. Boo loses big time again and now avoids his landlord, his neighbors, and his friends because he owes everybody money.

A boy (or it could be a girl) decides that he is tired of having to obey his parents, packs an overnight bag, and moves out when the coast is clear. He wanted his freedom and dreamed of the day when he could be his own boss. Once he is in charge of his own life, he'll call the shots and make all of the decisions. No more interruptions. No more making beds. No more emptying garbage. As a matter of fact, no more anything of real structure. He soon begins to miss what he had but is too proud to admit his mistakes. Like the prodigal son, he soon finds himself in need: "When he came to his senses, he said, 'How many of my father's hired servants have food to spare, and here I am starving to death! I will set out and go back to my father and say to him: Father, I have sinned against heaven and against you. I am no longer worthy to be called your son; make me like one of your hired servants'" (Luke 15:17-19). He has more hours in a day than he can actually handle. He begins to wish for instructions, but that pride of the flesh will not allow him to give in.

This is the warning that Jesus gave to as many as were willing to take advice from him. This warning is for our benefit. False prophets have a threefold purpose when they approach us. Just like their father (the devil), they come to "steal and kill and destroy" (John 10:10). After all, only a fool will work against his father. False prophets are imposters. They hide their true faces behind masks. Satan really wants our honor, trust, loyalty, and devotion. "Again, the devil took him to a very high mountain and showed him all the kingdoms of the world and their splendor. 'All this I will give you,' he said, 'if you will bow down and worship me.' Jesus said to him, 'Away from me, Satan! For it is written: Worship the Lord your God, and serve him only'" (Matthew 4:8-10). Satan is still fuming at God for kicking him out of heaven and does everything in his power to drive a wedge between God and his children.

Satan is not some six-foot-tall guy dressed in a red suit and holding a pitchfork. This devil is high tech. He wears the finest suits, drives the nicest automobiles, and doesn't take a backseat to anyone. He lives in the best places in town. He can speak any language. He relates to people at every level in life. He can preach until you feel like getting your praise on. He can shout, pull a crowd together, and build a major house. He has sweet-talked many people and made them think that they were a match for him. Don't play this devil cheap. He can cost a person his life. Throughout the scriptures, there is case after case of people who attempted to handle the devil without the assistance of the Lord. Most often, these people knew the will of God but thought that they could win on their own. Eve (Genesis 3:1-23), Balak (Numbers 22), Sampson (Judges 16), the man of God who listened to a lying prophet (1 Kings 13), Solomon (1 Kings 11:1-14)—each tried to swing things on his or her own and failed. These people clearly knew right from wrong but went contrary to what was revealed to them by the Lord.

Think about the many people who have lost their lives because they permitted the enemy to sell them a bill of rotten goods. Every few years or so another leader surfaces and leads masses of people into a dead-end road. Jim Jones is one of many imposters who sticks out in my mind

People like Jim Jones start off with an innocent front but often end in great sorrow. Many of them wrongfully interpret the scriptures to add authenticity to their cause but end up as dictators. People by the hundreds flock to these leaders in hopes of finding comfort, security, and the answers to many of life's complexities. Throughout the ages, people have been deceived into thinking that there are easy answers to difficult questions, only to discover that there aren't any. Although new faces and names are given, in reality, it is the same old stuff—lies and deceit.

False Predictors Will Come

Speaking to the people of Israel who were in exile in Babylon, the Lord said to them, "Do not let the prophets and diviners among you deceive you. Do not listen to the dreams you encourage them to have. They are prophesying lies to you in my name. I have not sent them," declares the Lord (Jeremiah 29:8-9).

One of the first cults that I paid any real attention to was the Peoples Temple (a.k.a. Jonestown). On November 18, 1978, more than 900 people died in Jonestown, Guyana, along with their leader, Jim Jones. This group was born in 1955 and called the Wings of Deliverance and later Peoples Temple. Jones reached out to all nationalities. And as he moved from Indiana to California and later out of the United States and into South America, so did many of the families in his congregation. Jones first made use of the Bible, however, later he put the Bible down and relied on Satan's lies. Soon afterward, many people realized that Jones was off base. By then, it was too late for them to back out; they were trapped at Jonestown in Guyana. Relatives and other concerned people grew so worried that it attracted national attention. Peoples Temple members were prisoners in a foreign land.

Long story short, Jones ordered everyone into the open-air pavilion, where they would die. The total count was 914, including 276 children. Jones was a strategist and a false prophet. He convinced people to give up their rights and place their complete confidence in him. Jones did as his father (Satan) ordered him to do. Satan's plan is to kill, steal, and destroy. Once the enemy isolates you from the truth and from others who know the truth, no one can hear you when you cry.

There are cases after cases of individuals who prey upon the innocent and the gullible. Their targets are not just those who don't know what they believe but also those who know very little about what they should believe. There are modern-day false prophets and groups who claim to know when the world will end. Many have selected specific days. Some thought the world would end as we approached the year 2000.

More recently, Harold Camping, who served as an American Christian radio broadcaster. Camping, president of Family Radio, a California-based radio station group that spans more than 150 markets in the United States, predicted the end of the world would occur on May 21, 2011. It should be noted that this prediction was not true.

The scriptures assure us that "no one knows about that day or hour, not even the angels in heaven, nor the Son, but only the Father" (Matthew 24:36).

There have always been people who claim to have special revelation and new insights from God as it concerns the future. Readers and advisors are more prevalent today than ever before. I am not sure which group disturbs me more, the psychics on television or the psychics in the local congregations who put words in God's mouth. At least on television, they offer a disclaimer in very small print: "for entertainment purposes only."

People Are Hungry For Secret Knowledge

If you have a voice, you can get a following. Someone will listen and follow you no matter where you are headed. Whenever someone prophesies and tells people what they want to hear, the response from the lips of many "church folks" is "praise God, I receive that." I am convinced that some people dislike having to think for themselves and prefer others to do their thinking for them. They don't want to work through their problems; they want a quick fix. They don't want to wait on God; they want microwave answers.

To get these quick fixes, they must ignore reality, soundness, intelligence, and, ultimately, God himself. They must go against everything they know to be the absolute truth. That was Eve's mistake. She knew what God had instructed her to do and not to do. Instead of following God's guidelines, she chose to take the advice of a stranger. This stranger promised her paradise. This stranger put Eve on a roller coaster, and she couldn't get off. This stranger was so smooth, Eve's own speech began to sound foreign to her ears, and yet, she failed to do anything about it. "'You will not certainly die,' the serpent said to the woman" (Genesis 3:4). I can imagine Eve asking herself, "No death for disobeying God?"

> I will be in a position to know good from evil and become a god at no cost to me? This is great, I can live with this. This is an opportunity to be my own person. Who will really know if I eat from this tree? This nice serpent told me that nothing would happen other than those good things he promised to me as a reward. I believe this new friend of mine. I know what God has said and that seems too confining for me. What the serpent told me is so much easier. I can grow in this program. This is my choice and it feels good to me. Mr. Serpent, sign me up."

I'm wondering, how far are we from this rationale today? Are we not equally guilty of these thought patterns with respect to our disobedience to God?

Satan tried this same trick with Jesus shortly after his fast of forty days and forty nights. Satan had a date with Jesus. Matthew 4:1 tells us, "Then Jesus was led by the Spirit into the wilderness to be tempted by the devil," who propositioned him to buy into the same program that Adam and Eve did. Jesus did not rely upon his own flesh to handle Satan. Jesus used the Word of God. Satan is not just a little guy who guesses at how to pull people down. Satan does his homework. If people insist upon using carnal weapons in the war against Satan, they will continue to be powerless against him. We need the Lord's help at all times; the Gospel of John explains the realities of the Lord Jesus Christ:

> I am the true vine, and my Father is the gardener. He cuts off every branch in me that bears no fruit, while every branch that does bear fruit he prunes so that it will be even more fruitful. You are already clean because of the word I have spoken to you. Remain in me, as I also remain in you. No branch can bear fruit by itself; it must remain in the vine. Neither can you bear fruit unless you remain in me. I am the vine; you are the branches. If you remain in me and I in you, you will bear much fruit; apart from me you can do nothing. If you do not remain in me, you are like a branch that is thrown away and withers; such branches are picked up, thrown into the fire and burned. If you remain in me and my words remain in you, ask whatever you wish, and it will be done for you. This is to my Father's glory, that you bear much fruit, showing yourselves to be my disciples. (John 15: 1-8)

Week after week, people on television and radio, as well as a few people that I know, claim to have the power to destroy Satan. They claim to have the ability to personally rebuke Satan, stomp him in the head, give him a black eye, and break his collar bone and the authority from God to tear Satan's kingdom down. Despite their attempts, Satan remains Satan. Satan gets a big laugh off of people who make inaccurate assessments about him. Jesus said that we make these errors because we do not know the Scriptures (Matthew 22:29).

How can you or anyone else harm this spirit? How can a person punch, kick, or destroy what is not seen? When will people realize that Satan is too clever for us to handle? Jesus said, "I am the vine; you are the branches. If a man remains in me and I in him, he will bear much fruit; apart from me you can do nothing"

(John 15:5). We need the Lord all the time. Note the spiritual intelligence Jesus used when Satan was trying to tempt him. Each time Satan attacked Jesus with temptation, Jesus relied upon the word of God as his defense: "It is written: Man shall not live on bread alone . . . It is written: Worship the Lord your God and serve him only . . . It is said: Do not put the Lord your God to the test" (Luke 4:4, 8, 12).

If we truly desire to be victorious against the tricks of Satan, we must do as Jesus did. There is power in the Word of God if we would read it, memorize it, meditate upon it, and practice it daily. God's word is a weapon for the true child of God. His word is a two-edged sword according to Hebrews 4:12. James gives us the proper way to be victorious when Satan is on the prowl. We are told to submit to God and resist the devil, and he will flee from us. Then we are to continue drawing near to God, and he in turn will draw near to us (James 4:7-8).

Finally, do not play with the devil because he is not a toy that can be picked up and dropped at will. The devil will always take you farther than you want to go, cost you more than you can afford, and entertain you longer than you want to stay. Jesus used the Word, and Satan couldn't hang around any longer. When used properly, the Word of God will enable any person to stand against this devil called Satan:

> Finally, be strong in the Lord and in his mighty power. Put on the full armor of God, so that you can take your stand against the devil's schemes. For our struggle is not against flesh and blood, but against the rulers, against the authorities, against the powers of this dark world and against the spiritual forces of evil in the heavenly realms. Therefore put on the full armor of God, so that when the day of evil comes, you may be able to stand your ground, and after you have done everything, to stand. Stand firm then,

> with the belt of truth buckled around your waist, with the breastplate of righteousness in place, and with your feet fitted with the readiness that comes from the gospel of peace. In addition to all this, take up the shield of faith, with which you can extinguish all the flaming arrows of the evil one. Take the helmet of salvation and the sword of the Spirit, which is the word of God. And pray in the Spirit on all occasions with all kinds of prayers and requests. With this in mind, be alert and always keep on praying for all of the Lord's people (Ephesians 6:10-18).

Use God's Word; it works.

CHAPTER 4

Some Things You Don't Need to See

When the woman saw that the fruit of the tree was good for food and pleasing to the eye, and also desirable for gaining wisdom, she took some and ate it. She also gave some to her husband, who was with her, and he ate it. (Genesis 3:6)

- Why aren't we content with what God has given to us?
- Why can't we trust that the Lord knows what is best for us?
- Why aren't we more content with where God has placed us?
- Why are we so easily swayed and influenced by outsiders to rebel against those who truly care for us, whether they are our parents, spouses, supervisors, teachers, team leaders, guardians, or pastors?

Many years ago I glanced at a Ziggy comic strip. Ziggy was running, and his friend caught up with him and asked where he was going. Ziggy replied, "Nowhere." His friend then asked, "Why are you running so fast"? There are a lot of Ziggies in the world today. They are in a hurry to go nowhere. The older community tries to warn the youngsters to take their time to grow up because they will be adults longer than they are children. Our parents and other mature people knew the negative effects that alcohol, tobacco, drugs, bad company, premarital sexual intercourse, and street life would have on young people. Their informing us was their way of seeking to preserve our young, tender lives. They wanted us to grow up in stable environments, get a quality education, earn respectable incomes, and make worthwhile contributions to our society. In other words, these folks wanted us to live long and not die prematurely. They did not want us to make excuses for not achieving the best out of life.

God Is Protective of Us

> He who dwells in the shelter of the Most High will rest in the shadow of the Almighty. I will say of the Lord, "He is my refuge and my fortress, my God, in whom I trust." Surely he will save you from the fowler's snare and from the deadly pestilence. He will cover you with his feathers, and under his wings you will find refuge; his faithfulness will be your shield and rampart. You will not fear the terror of night, nor the arrow that flies by day, nor the pestilence that stalks in the darkness, nor the plague that destroys at midday. A thousand may fall at your side, ten thousand at your right hand, but it will not come near you. You will only observe with your eyes and see the punishment of the wicked. If you make the Most High your dwelling—even the Lord, who is my refuge—then no harm will befall you, no disaster will come near your tent. For he will command his angels concerning you to guard you in all your ways . . . (Psalm 91:1-11)

God has always looked out for us and at the same time offered protection for us. The eye is very important. Through the eye come vision, ideas, and aspirations. The eye serves as the window to the soul. "The eye is the lamp of the body. If your eyes are healthy, your whole body will be full of light. But if your eyes are unhealthy, your whole body will be full of darkness. If then the light within you is darkness, how great is that darkness!" (Matthew 6:22-23).

Whatever we imagine within our hearts and are able to form its vision in our eyes, we will find some way to generate it. Distance is not a barrier for what we want. Cost is not a real problem, because if we don't have the money, we will borrow it. No obstruction will keep us from obtaining what we are able to see. This lesson comes early in the eleventh chapter of Genesis. People were concerned about making a name for themselves and sought to build a skyscraper. The Trinity convened, and the "Lord said, 'If as one people speaking the same language they have begun to do this, then nothing they plan to do will be impossible for them'" (Genesis 11:6).

> Now the whole world had one language and a common speech. As people moved eastward they found a plain in Shinar and settled there. They said to each other, "Come, let's make bricks and bake them thoroughly." They used brick instead of stone, and tar for mortar. Then they said, "Come, let us build ourselves a city, with a tower that reaches to the heavens, so that we may make a name for ourselves; otherwise we will be scattered over the face of the whole earth." But the Lord came down to see the city and the tower the people were building. The Lord said, "If as one people speaking the same language they have begun to do this, then nothing they plan to do will be impossible for them. Come, let us go down and confuse their language so they will not understand each other." So the Lord scattered them from there over all the earth, and they stopped building the city. (Genesis 11:1-8)

Little did this group know that they were somebody already because God made them somebody. They already had names for themselves.

Why did they think it necessary to be more than what God intended for them to be? Perhaps something or someone convinced them that they should do more to demonstrate their independence from God their creator. Why weren't these groups more grateful about what God had provided? Why couldn't they wait on the Lord to open new doors for them? Why did they devalue their places in the world? Why must we repeat history?

First, I think this group devalued their places because they were competing with each other. Competitive spirit is an ongoing problem almost everywhere you look. It is seen in the church on a regular basis. Too little time is spent cultivating friendships, relationships, and family ties. Too much time is spent spying on one another and reporting the findings to opposing parties. We are sinful by nature and selfish by practice. In Psalm 51:5, David informs us that we were born and shaped in iniquity. Paul informs us of our willful ignorance in Romans 1:21-23: "For although they knew God, they neither glorified him as God nor gave thanks to him, but their thinking became futile and their foolish hearts were darkened. Although they claimed to be wise, they became fools and exchanged the glory of the immortal God for images made to look like a mortal human being and birds and animals and reptiles."

Second, I find it difficult to thank the Lord for what he has given to me when, in my heart, I feel he should have given me more. God is a giving God who gives to us freely, "that you may be children of your Father in heaven. He causes his sun to rise on the evil and the good, and sends rain on the righteous and the unrighteous" (Matthew 5:45). Instead of showing our gratitude, we immediately compare what we have to what our neighbor has. After close scrutiny, we conclude that our neighbor's gift, talent, ability, home, spouse, job, church building . . . is better than ours. This comparison becomes the reason we seek something more than, or at least equal to, what the other person has. What we are saying to the Lord is, "You know, Lord, you could have done better by me. I'm insulted."

The third piece of this problem is that these people will not wait for the Lord to open doors for them. They are of the opinion that the Lord is holding something back from them, and they decide to go after it on their own. They are curious; they want to know. They have inquiring minds and will not rest until they are satisfied. They are going to show God that they can do what they want to do without his assistance. It is amazing that at the beginning of the twenty-first century, people are not any further in their faith in God's provisions than were those others who built the tower back in the day, after the flood. Have you met people who claim to have faith in God but make statements such as, "If God wants my trust, he must show me what is going to happen first." Are they like doubting Thomas, who said in essence, seeing is believing: "Now Thomas (also known as Didymus), one of the Twelve, was not with the disciples when Jesus came. So the other disciples told him, 'We have seen the Lord!' But he said to them, 'Unless I see the nail marks in his hands and put my finger where the nails were, and put my hand into his side, I will not believe'" (John 20:24-25).

The Bible reminds us of the impossibility of pleasing God without faith: "And without faith it is impossible to please God, because anyone who comes to him must believe that he exists and that he rewards those who earnestly seek him" (Hebrews 11:6).

<u>We Are Commanded to Walk with Faith</u>

The Bible instructs the people of God not to depend upon what we can see, but rather to walk by faith (2 Corinthians 5:7). And at the same time the Bible bids us to trust in the Lord with our full hearts: "Trust in the Lord with all your heart and lean not on your own understanding; in all your ways submit to him, and he will make your paths straight" (Proverbs 3:5-6). Now, what part of "walk by faith, not by sight" don't we get? Perhaps it's the faith issue. We don't mind attaching the word "faith" to our walk. In other words, we want to trust the Lord on our own terms because the parameters he sets are too narrow for us to walk within. We maintain that we know what is best for us. This is very foolish on our part, because it means that we miss out on the beauty of walking in the light of God and on having the companionship of a loving God walking beside us.

In one of the darkest hours of her life, after the tragic drowning of her husband, Louisa M. R. Stead, 1850-1917, a young mother, wrote, despite her tear-stained eyes, the words of this well-known hymn in 1882:

> 'Tis so sweet to trust in Jesus,
> Just to take him at his word;
> Just to rest upon his promise;
> Just to know "Thus saith the Lord."
>
> Jesus, Jesus, how I trust him!
> How I've proved him o'er and o'er!
> Jesus, Jesus, precious Jesus!
> O for grace to trust him more.

After wrestling with Satan over the issue of whether God was fair and generous, Eve finally was convinced that she was missing out on something special and that she could get it without the help of God. Satan hissed, "Look at this tree, girl. Doesn't it look good to you?" Eve yielded to the tempter, took another look at the tree, and concluded that the tree was good for food. Using my imagination, I can hear Eve's thoughts: "Oh, boy, this tree will make me wise. I will know the things that God knows. I will be Mrs. It! I will be a god also. People will look up to me and recognize me for the person that I truly am. I will really be a woman without God's help. I will be complete".

Not only did Eve eat of the tree, she gave some to her husband, and he ate too. Adam knew that Eve crossed the line. She was aggressive and assertive with her husband. She probably told him, "This will give us our independence. We can call our own shots from now on. Adam, just look at the benefits we will have. Everything will be different for us." Unfortunately, everything did change for this first human couple and not for the better, but for the worst.

Satan Creates a Hunger in People

It is important to note that, according to Genesis 2:9, the tree was in the center of the garden. This tree was the tree of "the knowledge of good and evil," i.e., everything. I am convinced that Eve and Adam had to travel a distance to get to this tree. If you let me tell the story my way, I would suggest to you that Adam and Eve had to pack a lunch because of the distance and time it took to get to the middle of the garden. Remember this fact about Satan: he doesn't have the authority to make us do wrong. He can, however, make friendly suggestions to us. He is in business to tempt us, and he is good at his job. Satan can't compel us to eat, so he convinces us that we are hungry for what he has in his pantry. The real question we must ask ourselves is, "Why are we so attracted to that which is off-limits to us?" Why must we run through the red light? Why do we travel deeper into debt just because someone mailed us a preapproved credit card with a $3,000 limit? Why do we keep sinning when we know that sinning is wrong? Do we really think God is unaware of what we are doing? And why is it necessary for us to cast the blame elsewhere when confronted by others or convicted by the Holy Spirit?

In the Bible, James gives us the correct perspective on what took place with Adam and Eve and what happens to us at the moment of our sinful activities:

> When tempted, no one should say, "God is tempting me." For God cannot be tempted by evil, nor does he tempt anyone; but each one is tempted when, by his own evil desire, he is dragged away and enticed. Then after desire has conceived, it gives birth to sin; and sin, when it is full-grown, gives birth to death. (James 1:13-15)

Sin makes many promises of pleasure to us. We usually want to believe that sin will deliver what it promises, but deep in our hearts we know that sin is a killer. Sin promises pleasure, but gives us pain. It promises prosperity, but gives us poverty. It promises peace, but we end up in war. It gives the impression that you will be happy, but it will leave you in your room isolated and in misery. Sin is very tricky. According to Hebrews 11:25, Moses opted out of being called the son of Pharaoh's daughter and made a conscience decision to suffer with God's people rather than enjoy the pleasures of sin, because he knew that those pleasures would not be blessed by God, and, they would be temporarily enjoyed. In considering the pleasures associated with sinful behavior, Solomon asks several questions:

> Who has woe? Who has sorrow? Who has strife? Who has complaints? Who has needless bruises? Who has bloodshot eyes? Those who linger over wine, who go to sample bowls of mixed wine. Do not gaze at the wine when it is red, when it sparkles in the cup, when it goes down smoothly! In the end it bites like a snake and poisons like a viper. Your eyes will see strange sights and your mind imagine confusing things. (Proverbs 23:29-33)

> Wine is a mocker and beer a brawler; whoever is led astray by them is not wise. (Proverbs 20:1)

Sin is dangerous, and it works against us. The only deliverance for the person who is enjoying the pleasures of sin comes from repentance. Sin appears good, but it isn't good. Sin is ugly. All sin is unrighteous, according to 1 John 5:17. There is nothing cute or innocent about sin. Sin is very expensive. Sin is calculating. It encourages you to plot your own way out of trouble if you get caught, while at the same time, assures you that you are completely safe. Sin suggests that no one will find out. But Moses said, ". . . and you may be sure that your sin will find you out" (Numbers 32:23).

We may get by for a season but, rest assured, your times of accountability are coming. The Bible reminds us that what we put out will come back to us and at the least expected time: "Do not be deceived: God cannot be mocked. A man reaps what he sows" (Galatians 6:7).

Is This What You Were Dying to See?

When thinking sound thoughts, no one truly desires to be in pain. No one welcomes punishment, misery, sorrow, or death. Whether we like to admit it or not, these negative emotions come to us because of our exposure to sin. The first man Adam was responsible for the sin we are born in. And because of his sin, all people are born in sin. The good news to this sin issue is found in the person of the "last man Adam", which is the Lord Jesus Christ according to the following passages.

> So it is written: "The first man Adam became a living being"; the last Adam, a life-giving spirit. The spiritual did not come first, but the natural, and after that the spiritual. The first man was of the dust of the earth; the second man is of heaven. This last man was made a quickening spirit. (1 Corinthians 15:45-47)

> For if, by the trespass of the one man, death reigned through that one man, how much more will those

> who receive God's abundant provision of grace and of the gift of righteousness reign in life through the one man, Jesus Christ! (Romans 5:17)

In the words of song poet Elvina Hall who penned the words to "Jesus Paid it All" in 1865

"I hear the Savior say, thy strength indeed is small," "Child of weakness, watch and pray, find in me thine all in all. Jesus paid it all. All to him I owe. Sin has left a crimson stain. He washed it white as snow."

Perhaps it is arrogance on our part as humans to expect successful outcomes while knowingly engaging in sinful behavior. It is clear that the wages of our personal and deliberate sin result in death. Romans 6:23 puts it so much better than I can: "For the wages of sin is death, but the gift of God is eternal life in Christ Jesus our Lord."

CHAPTER 5

I Was Afraid

> But the Lord called to the man, "Where are you?" He answered, "I heard you in the garden, and I was afraid because I was naked; so I hid." (Genesis 3:9-10)

What Are You Afraid Of?

Fear is an internal emotion that is usually caused by something external and sets off a person's alarm. The alarm is the end result of a break in the personal circuit, a warning that something is out of order. A person does not have to possess any special qualifications to be afraid. Fear is not restricted to any single class of people. All it takes for a person to fear is to be human. Being able to differentiate up from down, in from out, good from evil, and the like qualifies you to be able to fear. No one has to introduce us to fear; it is now a permanent part of human life by virtue of sin.

Fear is found among the young, middle aged, and older adults. Fear is common to the rich and powerful, and to the poor. Those who possess little to no education and those who have extensive higher learning are all familiar with fear. No particular race or cultures are exempt. Fear is not something that is only felt by the unsaved, because the Bible often reminds the people of God to "fear not":

After this, the word of the Lord came to Abram in a vision: "Do not be afraid, Abram. I am your shield, your very great reward. (Genesis 15:1)

"It's all right," he said. "Don't be afraid. Your God, the God of your father, has given you treasure in your sacks; (Genesis 43:23)

Then the Lord said to Joshua, "Do not be afraid; do not be discouraged. Take the whole army with you, and go up and attack Ai. For I have delivered into your hands the king of Ai, his people, his city and his land. (Joshua 8:1)

I said to you, "I am the Lord your God; do not worship the gods of the Amorites, in whose land you live." But you have not listened to me. (Judges 6:10)

And now, my daughter, don't be afraid. I will do for you all you ask. All the people of my town know that you are a woman of noble character. (Ruth 3:11)

Say to him, "Be careful, keep calm and don't be afraid. Do not lose heart because of these two smoldering stubs of firewood—because of the fierce anger of Rezin and Aram and of the son of Remaliah." (Isaiah 7:4)

So do not fear, for I am with you; do not be dismayed, for I am your God. I will strengthen you and help you; I will uphold you with my righteous right hand . . . But now, this is what the Lord says—he who created you, Jacob, he who formed you, Israel: "Do not fear, for I have redeemed you; I have summoned you by name; you are mine. (Isaiah 41:10, 43:1)

> Do not be afraid of those who kill the body but cannot kill the soul. Rather, be afraid of the one who can destroy both soul and body in hell. (Matthew 10:28)
>
> But the angel said to them, "Do not be afraid. I bring you good news that will cause great joy for all the people." (Luke 2:10)
>
> Do not be afraid of what you are about to suffer. I tell you, the devil will put some of you in prison to test you, and you will suffer persecution for ten days. Be faithful, even to the point of death, and I will give you life as your victor's crown. (Revelation 2:10)

In other words, a person can be saved, baptized, filled with the Holy Ghost, talented, gifted, and deeply in love with Jesus and yet be a victim of fear. Fear is mankind's enemy and is often unavoidable. Fear latches on to a person and will overstay its visit. Fear is knowledgeable. It knows where we live. Fear knows our telephone numbers, pager numbers, and e-mail and mailing addresses. Fear will find us wherever we go because fear is internal.

Fear will surface anywhere people are found. You can be at home, church, work, on vacation, or on a date, and fear will show up. Fear is not restricted to certain times, dates, and places. Fear will show up during celebrations and make its presence known. Fear is so great that others often accept our fears as their own and become co-owners of the fear with us. I believe there are two different schools of thought on this subject: Should Be University (SBU) and What Is University (WIU).

Should Be University

Many, if not all, people are pretty good at "what should be" in life. In this school, generally we speak from a position of privilege and many times at the expense of others. In this school, people speak volumes of what should and shouldn't take place. In this school, both the saved and the unsaved speak with great authority concerning what should be. They hold bragging rights, and rightly so; they are the alumni of SBU. According to these graduates, there is a list of things that should take place in the world today:

- People should get along with each other.
- People should trust, love, and honor everyone, no matter what their nationalities are.
- Neither personal status, the type of home they live in, educational level, nor bank accounts should separate us.
- Spouses should not argue and fight. They should remain at peace with each other until they die.
- Children should not be punished or given a curfew.
- There should be no pain, disease, sickness, or disappointments in anyone's life.
- There should be no deadly diseases.
- Peace should abide throughout the land and the sea.
- When attending the local church, the pastor should not make people feel as if they are doing wrong. After all, we are only human. He should just tell us that God loves us and understand that we cannot all be perfect.
- Every day should be perfect; no more rainstorms, tornadoes, snow blizzards or earthquakes.
- A person should not have to go to church and do what is right just to get into heaven.
- And finally, hell should not exist.

As you may have figured out by now, numerous students attended this university. People from every walk of life and every culture have either attended this school, are continuing their studies, or will enroll in it soon. Suffice it to say, these people reside at a great distance from reality. As children might say, "They are missing a few French fries from their Happy Meals." SBU students are missing a necessary component in their assessments about life. If you asked them about their contributions to the world, given the complexities of life, they would probably tell you that they want nothing to do with predicaments created by someone else. These people, however, need to see the larger picture. They need to understand what life was meant to be. Unfortunately, very few people enroll in WIU.

What Is University

WIU is less prestigious than SBU. The enrollment in this school is always small in comparison. The students excel in life despite their problems. They have come to grips with the reality of life's ups and downs. They hardly ever refer to SBU because they are realists. They have matured and are now sinking their teeth into the tough steak of life. You won't hear WIU students complaining about life's trials, hurts, and disappointments. They simply move into a realm of acceptance and roll with the punches. In his sermons, Reinhold Niebuhr used a well-known prayer, which has been quoted on many occasions. It is known as the Serenity Prayer. He prayed, "God, grant me the serenity to accept the things I cannot change, the courage to change the things I can, and the wisdom to know the difference."

WIU students reasonably understand the principles in life. Their understanding about life's issues is not predicated upon whether or not they have been saved. They know that at times they will be on a high, and at other times will be low. There will be moments of confidence and moments of ambivalence. Some days they may experience peace and at other times, upheaval. We each have these days and are able to relate to the realities in this life as we know them.

My mother had many sayings, some of which were not original. One was, "Into each life some rain must fall, but the sun will shine after while." I'm not sure of the origin of this statement, but it is true. Although this statement is not biblical, its sentiment lies in the Bible. As the psalmist said, "For his anger lasts only a moment, but his favor lasts a lifetime; weeping may stay for the night, but rejoicing comes in the morning" (Psalm 30:5).

If you want to be victorious in this life, you had better enroll in WIU. This school will keep you in touch with what is real and what is artificial. Many characters in the Bible attended WIU.

> There is a time for everything, and a season for every activity under heaven: a time to be born and a time to die, a time to plant and a time to uproot, a time to kill and a time to heal, a time to tear down and a time to build, a time to weep and a time to laugh, a time to mourn and a time to dance, a time to scatter stones and a time to gather them, a time to embrace and a time to refrain, a time to search and a time to give up, a time to keep and a time to throw away, a time to tear and a time to mend, a time to be silent and a time to speak, a time to love and a time to hate, a time for war and a time for peace. (Solomon in Ecclesiastes 3:1-8)
>
> I know that nothing good lives in me, that is, in my sinful nature. For I have the desire to do what is good, but I cannot carry it out. For what I do is not the good I want to do; no, the evil I do not want to do this I keep on doing. Now if I do what I do not want to do, it is no longer I who do it, but it is sin living in me that does it. So I find this law at work: When I want to do good, evil is right there with me. For in my inner being I delight in God's law; but I see another law at work in the members of my body, waging war against the law of my mind and making me a prisoner of the law of sin at work within my members. What a wretched man I am! Who will rescue me from this body of death? Thanks be to God—through Jesus Christ our Lord! So then, I myself in my mind am a

> slave to God's law, but in the sinful nature a slave to the law of sin. (The apostle Paul in Romans 7:18-25)

Speaking to his disciples, who had vowed to be with him all the way, Jesus said:

> But a time is coming, and has come, when you will be scattered, each to his own home. You will leave me all alone. Yet I am not alone, for my Father is with me. I have told you these things, so that in me you may have peace. In this world you will have trouble. But take heart! I have overcome the world. (John 16:32-33)

<u>The Way It Was Meant to Be</u>

Six different times the Bible comments on God's attitude toward his work. In Genesis 1:4, 10, 12, 18, 21, and 25, we read, "And God saw that it was good." Some time following the Creation, there was a meeting among the God-head. Then God said, "Let us make man in our image, in our likeness . . ." (Genesis 1:27). Just think about this, God created us to resemble him.

God's personality has two main attributes. Through these characteristics, we have a better understanding of who God is and what God is like. The two attributes are morality and naturalness. Man was not created to take God's place, but he was created to be Godlike in character. God's moral attributes include love, kindness, patience, goodness, orderliness, and generosity:

> Love is patient, love is kind. It does not envy, it does not boast, it is not proud. It does not dishonor others, it is not self-seeking, it is not easily angered, it keeps no record of wrongs. Love does not delight in evil but rejoices with the truth. It always protects, always trusts, always hopes, always perseveres. Love never fails. But where there are prophecies, they will cease;

> where there are tongues, they will be stilled; where there is knowledge, it will pass away. (1 Corinthians 13:4-8)
>
> Whoever does not love does not know God, because God is love. (1 John 4: 8)

And he is also a God of wrath: "The wrath of God is being revealed from heaven against all the godlessness and wickedness of people, who suppress the truth by their wickedness" (Romans 1: 18).

God's natural attributes, in part, are his ability to be eternal, unchanging, and present everywhere at the same time. He is sovereign. Made in the image of God, we possess the ability to please him. Once God finished creating people and things, God saw that everything he did was good.

God placed the first couple, who he joined together, into his garden and gave to them clear and meaningful instructions. During this time period, everything (animals and nature) functioned properly. Among this couple, the animals, and nature itself, there were no problems. Life, at best, was simple. This couple was innocent. They had no pain, aches, fights, or concerns. There were no big "I"s nor little "You"s. The "me, myself, and I" syndrome did not exist. Adam and Eve were one in thought, fellowship, and friendship. And they were one with God. Their desire was to obey, worship, and praise God. There weren't any distractions to their devotion to God, such as we have. Today we use television, sports, mega-shopping malls, garage sales, second and third jobs, family, friends, homes, and gardens as excuses for not giving to God the glory due his name, particularly on Sunday.

Adam and Eve worshiped God without apology. They lived simple yet meaningful lives, uncomplicated by life's devices. And because of their loyalty to God, they enjoyed a stress-free lifestyle. They knew no guilt, anxiety, and most assuredly, they knew no fear. The however to this relationship between Adam and God is that something went sour in the garden that altered Adam's security. His boldness diminished, and he became frightened.

<u>Who Was Adam Afraid Of?</u>

Adam became afraid of the one in whose image he was created. Adam knew God intimately and was aware of why God created him. He was not ambivalent about his earthly assignment. He knew the voice of God and had no reason to ignore it. Adam knew that God was pleased with his creations. He knew of God's concern for his loneliness and that he was put to sleep by God so that he could perform the first surgery. God did not clone Adam. He did one better. God created a masterpiece and Adam called her woman. This woman became Adam's helpmate, according to Genesis 2:18. The couple rejected God's guidelines for living a righteous life and decided to follow the voice of a complete stranger, which brings two things to my mind.

The first is what is known today as the New Age Movement, as described in a pamphlet written by Dr. Dale A Robbins titled "The New Age Movement: What Christians Should Know. He shares with us information concerning what he calls

The Present New Age Movement

Today, the New Age movement appears to be a loose knit group of innocent organizations with ambiguous goals or leadership. But beneath the surface there is a definite, organized, secret leadership and strategy which guides the vast movement. The main body of leadership resides in an organization called "The Planetary Initiative For The World We Choose."

One of their most celebrated demonstrations of unity and public relations occurred on August 16-17, 1988. Over eighty million New Agers unified themselves for what was called the largest assembly of mass meditation in history. Widely reported by the news media, the "Harmonic Convergence," also referred to as the "Planetary Surrender," occurred simultaneously in nearly every nation and major city. Led and organized largely by 144,000 Shamans, witches, witch doctors and a whole assortment of New Age mystics, they joined in a period of meditation agreement for the release of "spiritual forces" which would bring about their desire for a "one world government and world religion." Only two years earlier, on December 31, 1986, a slightly smaller gathering of fifty million New Age adherents joined in meditation for the purpose to "alter the manner which humanity understands reality."

In actuality, these gatherings of meditation were acts of worship and service to the Devil. One can only imagine what kind of demons and evil spiritual forces were unleashed upon the world as witch doctors, shamans and mystics called upon the powers of darkness to distort humanity's perception of truth.

Is it no wonder that evil and wickedness has intensified in the world since that time? Think of the power of God that could be released if eighty million Christians combined their faith in one massive prayer meeting!

I believe this is what Satan was doing with the first couple in the garden. I believe he was setting up shop for his new world order.

The second thing is what the Apostle Paul called "wind of doctrine": "Then we will no longer be infants, tossed back and forth by the waves, and blown here and there by every wind of teaching and by the cunning and craftiness of people in their deceitful scheming" (Ephesians 4:14). Because of this wind, the couple thought they could handle life on their own terms.

Their disobedience led to disillusionment and fear of God. God did not abandon Adam and Eve, they abandoned God, which brought a tear in their fellowship with God.

I am convinced that Adam was afraid because he went where he was not permitted to go; as a result, his peace of mind, as well as the peace in his household, vanished. He was no longer sure about where he was going or even what he was doing. The only thing that stood out in Adam's mind was the contract he and Eve had signed with a stranger. The Adam who was once sure of himself was now under a cloud of doubt and fear. He could no longer make his mortgage payments and feared that God would show up at his used-to-be happy home. He may have entertained the thought that God would hate him for being disobedient. Fear had a sure grip on the couple, and it was eating them alive. I can almost see Adam and Eve looking for new sleeping quarters. They now feared a future of having to face the God who had created them in his own image.

Why Did Adam Say He Was Afraid?

The Bible answers this question. Indeed, Adam answers this question for us. He admits that he heard the voice of God in the garden (Genesis 3:10). Fear will cause people do things they did not know they were capable of doing. Adam had never before played hide-and-seek with God; he was always visible and worked with his hands on top of the table. Adam and Eve never had difficulty making noise in their worship and with their praise before the Lord. They never needed any filler or other artificial devices to praise the Lord. Why did they believe they needed a mediator? They'd never before needed to cover themselves with leaves to approach God. Why was it so difficult for them to welcome the presence of the Lord now?

The second thing we should note is that Adam had a logical reason to be afraid. He knew that he was accountable to God. Everything around the couple looked different. Even Eve no doubt seemed different to Adam. They both began to feel a slight draft. The covering—anointing, shield, protective covering—they once enjoyed from God had now ended. They no longer resembled the pure and innocent image of God as they once had. They'd lost what they had but thought that it could be replaced with a few leaves. "Then the eyes of both of them were opened, and they realized they were naked; so they sewed fig leaves together and made coverings for themselves" (Genesis 3:7). At that point, they decided to start a tailoring business and made matching outfits for themselves. Little did they realize that no amount of covering could hide their nakedness from the all-searching eyes of an all-wise God. "Nothing in all creation is hidden from God's sight. Everything is uncovered and laid bare before the eyes of him to whom we must give account" (Hebrews 4:13).

Third, Adam was afraid because of the penetrating question God asked of him: "But the Lord God called to the man, 'Where are you?'" (Genesis 3:9). I am sure this question reverberated in the hearts of Adam and Eve until they came out of hiding. Just for a moment, why not explore this question—where are you?—but replace Adam's name with your own. What do you now feel? How will you answer the question that God asked? God knew where Adam and Eve were, and he knows where we are today. God wanted Adam to give an account of where he was. His question led to a series of other questions, such as:

1. Where are you in view of where I have placed you?
2. Why are you no longer walking in the light I have provided for you?
3. Why do you hang your head down in shame?
4. Why are you avoiding me now?
5. Why are you questioning my love for you?
6. Why do you feel it necessary to seek shelter apart from that which I have I provided for you?

7. Why do you ignore me and encourage others to do likewise?

The Lord Jesus Christ is saying to each of us today, as he did to the church in Ephesus, "I know your deeds . . . Remember the height from which you have fallen! Repent and do the things you did at first. If you do not repent, I will come to you and remove your lamp stand from its place." (Revelation 2:2, 5) Where are you today? How will you respond to God's question? Are you afraid of God, in whose image you were made?

Fear is appropriate when one is engaging in unethical and impractical behavior. The one who makes a conscious choice to do wrong should be afraid. Recognizing, however, that we as Christians must appear before the judgment seat of Christ to give an account of our stewardship, whether our works are good or evil, should create wholesome fear in us all. "So we make it our goal to please him, whether we are at home in the body or away from it. For we must all appear before the judgment seat of Christ, so that each of us may receive what is due us for the things done while in the body, whether good or bad" (2 Corinthians 5: 9-10). The unsaved person should be afraid of dying in sin because eternal separation and punishment will be his lot:

> Then I saw a great white throne and him who was seated on it. The earth and the heavens fled from his presence, and there was no place for them. And I saw the dead, great and small, standing before the throne, and books were opened. Another book was opened, which is the book of life. The dead were judged according to what they had done as recorded in the books. The sea gave up the dead that were in it, and death and Hades gave up the dead that were in them, and each person was judged according to what they had done. Then death and Hades were

> thrown into the lake of fire. The lake of fire is the second death. Anyone whose name was not found written in the book of life was thrown into the lake of fire. (Revelation 20: 11-15)

An unhealthy fear arises when a person worries about when the world will end. It is unhealthy to get stressed out about what sicknesses or problems might come our way. Many people I know worried about the turning of the twenty-first century. Some were deeply concerned about what the new century and beyond would bring. An older married couple withdrew their life savings because they feared that there would be problems at banks in the year 2000. Unfortunately, someone watched them make the withdrawal, followed them home, and robbed them of every dollar. I do not believe the Lord wants us to live each day worrying about whether we will make it. That shows a lack of faith.

A healthy fear is a reverential fear of the Lord. As Solomon put it, "The fear of the Lord is the beginning of knowledge, but fools despise wisdom and instruction" (Proverbs 1:7). Our Lord instructs us not to think about tomorrow because we have enough to concern ourselves with today. He encourages us to place our trust in him rather than in man or devices. We would do well to lean on the same God that David leaned on, especially when our way gets dark and clouds of uncertainty arise. David reminds us that "the Lord is our light and salvation and asks 'Whom shall I fear?'" (Psalm 27:1).

In the meantime, remain in the light of God. Doing so will ensure a great fellowship with the Lord. "But if we walk in the light, as he is in the light, we have fellowship with one another, and the blood of Jesus, his Son, purifies us from every sin" (1 John 1:7).

> What a fellowship, what a joy divine,
> Leaning on the everlasting arms;
> What a blessedness, what a peace is mine,

Leaning on the everlasting arms.
O how sweet to walk in this pilgrim way,
Leaning on the everlasting arms;
O how bright the path grows from day to day,
Leaning on the everlasting arms.
What have I to dread, what have I to fear,
Leaning on the everlasting arms;
I have blessed peace with my Lord so near,
Leaning on the everlasting arms.
Leaning, leaning,
Safe and secure from all alarms,
Leaning, leaning,
Leaning on the everlasting arms.

—Elisha A. Hoffman, 1887

If we lean on the Lord and obey his every command, there will be no room for fear.

PART TWO

Today's Anxiety

CHAPTER 6

Don't Park It Down Here

> Do not store up for yourselves treasures on earth, where moth and rust destroy, and where thieves break in and steal. But store up for yourselves treasures in heaven, where moth and rust do not destroy, and where thieves do not break in and steal. For where your treasure is, there your heart will be also. (Matthew 6:19-21)

My good friend Ronald K. Hill served as executive director for the Baptist Global Mission Bureau for a number of years. While visiting our home, he once said to me in jest, "Winfrey, you are not going to want to go to heaven because that will mean leaving your home and all of these nice things behind." He was joking with me and at the same time paying us a compliment for having a nice and comfortable home. Now while I knew that he was joking with me, I also heard him loud and clear. I thought about the many people whose goal in life is to become so comfortable on earth, there is no real desire to leave it. The Lord has made all things good and with a purpose in mind. He has freely given some of us many things in this world, while at the same time permitting others to just view them. He intends for us to keep moving. What propels us to ignore the fact that we were not meant to remain on the face of the earth and be suspended throughout eternity in the prime of our lives? Why do we have trouble moving on? Why don't we acknowledge the "no parking" signs in life? We know too well what the consequences will be if we are caught, and yet, we break the law.

Who does not like the pleasant times in life? Pleasant times do not come that often, and when they do come, we try to hold on to them forever. We are by nature a very selfish people; we want what we want, when we want it. For a great number of people, cost is not the issue when it comes to having what they want. Many people long for the comforts in life even when it means spending beyond their ability to pay the price. What propels us to ignore the fact that we must keep moving? Self-deception is the number one cause for our faulty thinking. Too often we think that life should be easy and free from hurt, pain, and disappointment. We convince ourselves that we can claim the good in life and resist anything that is an obstacle to our plans. We become stuck and then invite others to support our feeble efforts to park in a "no parking" zone. Everyone loves conveniences in life. For instance, when we go to the mall or a favorite restaurant, we look for a parking place that ensures we will not have to walk very far to our destination.

How many times have you thought that you had found the perfect parking spot, only to see the sign for a fire hydrant, handicapped or senior parking, or a loading zone that states "no parking here"? Often when we see these signs, the pride in our hearts quickly comes to the surface. I can recall many occasions when there was an officer directing traffic, and I thought it was safe to park in a certain spot, but the officer indicated that I should keep moving. What did I do when I was told to move? I became upset at that officer for not allowing me to create my own parking rules. At times I have tried to reason with an officer, stating that I would only be parked for a short time. Of course, the officer told me to "move it or get ticketed."

At some airports, motorists are asked to drop their passengers off and keep moving. In my hometown, Chicago, if your automobile remains in front of the airport too long, you soon get a ticket. If you leave your car unattended, it may be ticketed and towed, and you will have to pay towing and storage fees. What part of "no parking" do we not understand?

In the same way, sometimes we get stuck in life and refuse to move on. How many people do you know who are like this? Life has moved on; their friends, associates, and family have all moved on; and yet they remain where they were when "the good life" was the order of the day. How many times have you asked yourself, "How come things can't remain as they once were?" Think of the many people who talk about their past and act as if it were their present state. Can't you hear them reflecting?

- I was once the top person on my job and everyone looked up to me . . .
- I was the CEO for XYZ Company, and I made the important decisions for the company . . .
- I always had everything I wanted and needed because my parents indulged me . . .
- I never had to beg for anything before in life; why should I beg now?
- I was once the leader of the choir in my church . . .
- Everyone used to come to me for advice . . .
- When I was the pastor of that church, I did things much differently . . .
- I am not sure why people do not recognize that I am the same person I have always been and that I have not changed just because I am older . . .
- I remember when I could eat anything I wanted to eat and not get indigestion . . .
- I have always been able to buy what I wanted whenever I wanted it . . .

Moving on seems to be a real challenge for many people, particularly given all of the inconveniences in life. Again, we want what we want, and when we want it. Moving on is not a part of our agenda. We want to suspend all of the rules and live on flowery beds of ease. To this end, we tend to build cases to justify why we should remain where we were years ago. How many parents and grandparents do you know who will not acknowledge that the years have moved on and have left them behind? Why do people tell themselves, "I still have all that I had years ago"? It's called self-deception. These people are stuck in the past and refuse to acknowledge their current situation. So many of them are in denial about their sicknesses, ages, and their statuses in life. They have a block on reality and seem to take issue with anyone who dares to escort them into reality. Rather than listening to reason, they prefer to fight for their past honor.

Why Can't We Just Let Go?

We do not let go of old accomplishments and the good old times because at one point in our life that was how we were identified. We were known for this, that, and the other. Now that we are at a new place in life and everything to us is new, we do not want to move on. We enjoy talking about what we once did and how we once made things work for us. We also are selfish because we do not want others to get the attention we once received. So we fight for our right to remain an idol in the eyes of the public. I am convinced that some people feel that no one will remember their past efforts, so they make a nuisance of themselves to get others to continue honoring them. We must come to grips with the reality that we only get to be on center stage at certain times in life; and then, it is time to step aside for the next rising star. Life can be like a seesaw. You can only be at the top when the other person is on the ground; when the tables turn, you must leave your high position to make way for the person on the other end of the seesaw.

There are beauty products designed to slow down the aging process. Pills, creams, surgeries, injections, and self-help books (in my opinion), competing for our time, energy, and finances. I don't think we will ever run out of people, companies, and manufacturers trying to sell us solutions for remaining young. Here is a testimonial I found online about one anti-aging product:

> The product . . . is used with enormous success by tens of thousands in the elimination of many diseases which the medical community label as "incurable" . . . I have witnessed patients dramatically improve, and in many cases, literally walk away from diseases and disorders altogether.

Many unfortunate and naïve individuals have been deceived by people and companies who prey on the unsuspecting. In many instances, those who were deceived finally came to the reality that their efforts had come to naught. After repeating some chants, taking some pills, doing physical gyrations, and even praying to the Lord to keep them young and beautiful, they still grew older, became sick, and faced death

Now on the other hand you can find some helpful hints and suggestions on things a person can do naturally to keep fit as they age. I find this list interesting and helpful:

Ten Ways to Stay Young

1. Drink six to eight glass of water every day.
2. Stretch and strengthen your legs.
3. Train the upper body.
4. Strengthen your abdominal muscles five times a week.
5. Do aerobic exercises.
6. Choose the best activities for enhancing brain power.
7. Breathe from your diaphragm.
8. Grill or steam your food.

9. Try colored vegetables.
10. Enjoy fresh fruit for dessert.

We should do whatever we can to preserve our bodies and stay in the very best of health. We should know our bodies, and live to ensure our good health.

<u>Jesus Knew What He Was Talking About</u>

> Jesus said, "Do not store up for yourselves treasures on earth, where moths and vermin destroy, and where thieves break in and steal. But store up for yourselves treasures in heaven, where moths and vermin do not destroy, and where thieves do not break in and steal. For where your treasure is, there your heart will be also." (Matthew 6:19-21)

Moths are a reality, as are other vermin. There once was a woman who did not believe in banks and decided to store her thousands of dollars in a box beneath her bed. One day she had a great need for her money, but she discovered that rodents had shredded her dollar bills to make nests for their young. Let me ask you: How many of your clothes bears the imprint of hangers or are full of dust because of a lack of use? Did you not know anyone (the less fortunate or homeless, a friend or family member) who would have appreciated the garments? How much food has spoiled because it just sat in the refrigerator or freezer? Could we not find some hungry person or a needy family to feed? In other words, Jesus is saying to us, "Make better use of the resources that I have allowed you to manage." Don't continue to just think of yourself; think about the plight of others. Solomon said, in his wisdom, "Do not withhold good from those to whom it is due, when it is in your power to act. Also, we are to consider the needs of others . . . Whoever is kind to the poor lends to the Lord, and he will reward them for what they have done" (Proverbs 3:27, 19:17).

Along this same line of thinking, do not hoard things just because you are able to afford them. A man's life does not consist of the accumulated things in his life: "Then he said to them, 'Watch out! Be on your guard against all kinds of greed; life does not consist in an abundance of possessions'" (Luke 12:15). We were never meant to have our treasures on display as trophies for others to admire. Whenever we brag too much, there is a thief outside, waiting for us to go to bed. They will break in and murder for the smallest items. Jesus says, in effect, make what you have accumulated in life count for all of eternity. Don't get caught holding nothing at the end of your journey; send your luggage ahead. Entrust your treasures to the capable hands of the Lord Jesus Christ. Don't park down here, because life at best is too short. You really don't know who to trust with your goods, and your hands are not strong enough to hold on to your belongings, so express them to heaven and trust them to the Lord's safe-keeping. If we can learn the art of letting go, we will be better off. Do you see the "no parking" sign? Are you illegally parked in a "no parking" zone? Are you wasting time arguing and justifying why you deserve to park where you are? If this is you, move your vehicle. And if you hate having to walk long distances in the parking lot, plan to arrive earlier next time.

CHAPTER 7

More than Food and Clothes

> Don't worry, saying, "What shall we eat?" or "What shall we drink?" or "What shall we wear?" For the pagans run after all these things, and your heavenly Father knows that you need them. (Matthew 6:31)

There must be a reason why we are discouraged due to our concerns about basic human needs such as food, water, and clothing. People throw out and waste more food and water than they make good use of. Many meals go uneaten simply because someone decides they don't eat a certain kind of food. If the garbage disposal doesn't eat the meal, it gets tossed in the trash. This is very unfortunate because world hunger is a serious matter.

> The world is facing a hunger crisis unlike anything it has seen in more than 50 years.
>
> 925 million people are hungry. Every day, almost 16,000 children die from hunger-related causes. That's one child every five seconds. There were 1.4 billion people in extreme poverty in 2005. The World Bank estimates that the spike in global food prices in 2008, followed by the global economic recession in 2009 and 2010 has pushed between 100-150 million people into poverty.

There are people, in this country and in others, who really know what it is like to be hungry and thirsty. They live in severe poverty. Truth be told, our garbage would seem like a banquet to them. The food and fresh water many of us waste would be heaven to those who are dying because they lack these precious resources. We also take shoes and clothing for granted. Many children request brand-name clothing and shoes; meanwhile, people in poor and desolate areas are walking around barefoot or with makeshift shoes. I saw in an email forwarded to me the picture (taken by Kate_A's photo stream) of an individual somewhere wearing two empty two-liter plastic bottles flattened to accommodate this person's feet. These bottles were used as footwear. And just the thought that a person would have to depend on this type of make-shift shoe is enough to let me know just how blessed we are to have shoes to wear.

As Americans, our need for these items is a learned behavior. We are consumed with greed because we are encouraged to have and to have more. We are barely satisfied with what we do have. We just always want more, more, and more. When was the last time you visited a buffet? Have you looked at some of those plates diners take away from the cold and warm trays? I have seen plates loaded with mountains of food and in a matter of minutes over half of it is tossed into the garbage bin. (Although, I admit that sometimes a particular food may be more appealing to the eye than it is to the palate.)

My siblings and I grew up poor and sometimes had small portions of food. At times, we did not want what we'd been given. We were reminded that there were children in Africa and in other foreign countries who were starving and would love to have our meals. The message was this: don't waste food.

Most Americans don't have to worry about what we were going to eat; our concern is whether we'll like it or not. Our second thought is often, what will we eat next? Reports on television and in articles and books describe countries where the drinking water is the same water people use to bathe, water the livestock, and where human elimination takes place. From time to time, remains of animals and humans float by, and I can hardly believe what my eyes behold. For these poor and disadvantaged people, there are no water-filtration systems. Drinking contaminated water is a means of survival. Water is so necessary and without it, one will dehydrate and can eventually die. In school we learned that water makes up 50 to 70 percent of the adult body weight. And due to the loss of this water, through urine and sweat, it must be replaced. Once dehydration sets in, the door is open to headaches, weariness, a lack of concentration, and life-threatening illnesses.

We also spend a lot of precious time deciding what we will wear. Many people dress to impress. If they are going to three different events that day, they will wear three different outfits. A few people will return home to change if they see someone else wearing the same outfit. We have become fashion bugs to the degree that we allow major department stores to tell us what we should wear in any given season. Stores are crowded because people want the image they see in catalogues and on television. Why must we have the latest fashions? Is there something wrong with the garments you purchased two months ago? Have you really outgrown those clothes, or are you seeking an excuse to get back into the mall so that you can keep up with the call for "new rags"?

How many people have closets stuffed with clothes they have never worn? How many of those items still have the price tags on them? How many times have you heard someone say, "I know I can't fit that garment, but I'm going to get back into it"? How many times have you seen someone who is unable to pay for clothing because he had insufficient money or his credit card was maxed out? Just a few weeks ago I was in the checkout line in a store. A woman was also in line. Each of the three credit cards she presented for payment were denied. She wanted what she had no visible means of paying for. I don't have to tell you the embarrassment that was plastered on this woman's face as she tried to speak softly to the cashier. To add insult to injury, after speaking to a customer-service representative on the phone, she was still denied the purchase.

Why are we so consumed with what we are going to eat, drink, and wear? I have a sneaky suspicion that there are several factors. One is personal gratification of the flesh. This is a selfish attitude that says "me first." We put blinders on when it comes to giving others a slice of the pie. As poet Samuel Butler said, "Self-preservation is the first law of nature."

In 1975 my son Marlon was born premature with a respiratory disorder and yellow with jaundice. He was very tiny and was confined to an incubator for a while until he gained some weight and the disorders cleared up. When Marlon came home and started on baby formula and the like, he never seemed to stop eating. The first time he walked unassisted was because he desired some pizza, and he didn't stop until he achieved his goal. As he grew older and began attending preschool, his regular question when he woke up was, "What are we going to eat, Daddy?" One morning I was hanging a ceiling-mounted light fixture for the kitchen. Marlon, at the age of four, kept looking at me and finally asked "Daddy, do you like toast?" I responded, "Yes, son." He said, "So do I." As I continued to get the screw in the heavy light fixture, Marlon continued to talk about this toast until I asked him if he wanted toast. His answer was yes. I came down from the ladder and fixed him the toast; he thanked me, and I got back on the ladder.

Just as I was lining up the screws with the holes, Marlon looked at me and asked his next question. "Daddy, do you like jelly on your toast?" At this point, I dropped one of the screws; now I was a bit hot under the collar. I got down from the ladder with the light fixture and got Marlon some jelly for his toast, but before I could get back on the ladder, Marlon poured a mountain of thanks on me for the toast and jelly. I thought that my son was satisfied, but he asked one last question; "Daddy, do you like eggs with your toast and jelly?" It finally sunk into my brain that this boy was hungry and if I wanted to hang that light, I had better feed him. I fixed him a complete breakfast, and he was satisfied and looked at me as though to say, "It took you long enough."

Eating and drinking are both essential for human survival and can also be linked to the "lusts of the flesh." I believe this is why Satan made his appeal to Jesus when he was in the wilderness. How convenient it was for Satan to approach Jesus just after he had fasted for forty days and nights and was hungry, talking about eating some bread. Satan no doubt decided on this plan since it had worked on Eve, Adam, and Esau:

> When the woman saw that the fruit of the tree was good for food and pleasing to the eye, and also desirable for gaining wisdom, she took some and ate it. She also gave some to her husband, who was with her, and he ate it. Then the eyes of both of them were opened, and they realized they were naked; so they sewed fig leaves together and made coverings for themselves. (Genesis 3:6-7)

> But Jacob said, "Swear to me first." So he swore an oath to him, selling his birthright to Jacob. Then Jacob gave Esau some bread and some lentil stew. He ate and drank, and then got up and left. So Esau despised his birthright. (Genesis 25:33-3)

Of course, Jesus was not tempted to compromise his standing with his father. When challenged to eat and therefore prostitute his integrity, Jesus fought back with the Word of God and told the tempter that "man did not live by bread alone, but by every word that proceeds from the mouth of God" (Matthew 4:4).

Clothing is necessary in our society. What is it that entices a person to lust for clothing? I am convinced that it is the lust of the flesh. People are heard saying "I just want to look good, and cost is not a factor." Looking nice in your clothes is not a bad thing. What is a bad thing is when are addicted to an over abundance of clothes. Gehazi is a classic example:

> Gehazi, the servant of Elisha, the man of God, said to himself, "My master was too easy on Naaman, this Aramean, by not accepting from him what he brought. As surely as the Lord lives, I will run after him and get something from him." So Gehazi hurried after Naaman. When Naaman saw him running toward him, he got down from the chariot to meet him. "Is everything all right?" he asked. "Everything is all right," Gehazi answered. "My master sent me to say, 'Two young men from the company of the prophets have just come to me from the hill country of Ephraim. Please give them a talent of silver and two sets of clothing.'" "By all means, take two talents," said Naaman. He urged Gehazi to accept them, and then tied up the two talents of silver in two bags, with two sets of clothing. He gave them to two of his servants, and they carried them ahead of Gehazi. When Gehazi came to the hill, he took the things from the servants and put them away in the house. He sent the men away, and they left. (2 Kings 5:20-2)

Gehazi lusted for clothing to the degree that he lied about the prophet Elisha in an attempt to look and feel good. One should never underestimate the power of lust. Lust is not limited to only one area of a person's life. Even when we know and understand the inappropriateness of what we lust for, something within us seems to override good sense and allows 'dumb' to take over. Lust has ruined the lives of many people in history. Great and small men alike have been ruined due to their lust for more. Kings, queens, lawyers, judges, principals, executives, pastors, and others in all walks of life have fallen because of their appetites. Jesus asked, "What good will it be for someone to gain the whole world, yet forfeit their soul? Or what can anyone give in exchange for their soul?" (Matthew 16:26).

The more material things some people have, the more powerful and in charge they feel. As one friend once remarked, "I bought my pastor a tool but I bought a much better one for myself." This is the "my car [or my home] is bigger than yours" mentality. Who really cares how big or how small the item is? What really matters is, does what you have work for you? Is it adequate for the job? If what you have will accomplish the desired results, then go for it and be at ease. We should not go through life competing with others. We would be much better off if only we would learn how to compliment or work in concert with others. The truth is, the more you own, the more you have to take care of. The less you own, the less you have to care for. Make life easy on yourself by living modestly. If affluence has complicated your life, push the stop button and get off that ride, because you may be headed for a great disappointment.

Discovering Bird Activity

> Look at the birds of the air; they do not sow or reap or store away in barns, and yet your heavenly Father feeds them. Are you not much more valuable than they? (Matthew 6:26)

While vacationing in Melbourne, Australia in 2010, my wife and I went on an excursion to the Yu Yang Regional Park. This is a wildlife area where we saw a few native animals. I especially wanted to see kangaroos in their natural environments. We first went on a hunt for koala bears. After that successful search, we then went in search for some wild kangaroos, which were in the Serendip Sanctuary, a different area.

The two areas had different species of birds. Each species was unique in itself. We were introduced to the magpie, bush-turkey, blue-faced parrot-finch, little kingfisher, and, later on, the emu; these were just a few of the birds. Their colors were brilliant and beautiful, and, like the birds in the United States, they all seemed to have one thing in common: they did not appear to be stressed out about anything. I did see one group of birds who defended their territory from egg thieves, but otherwise, these birds maintained their routine of moving from point A to point B. I thought to myself, *What a wonderful life these creatures have*.

In the Serendip Sanctuary, Roger, our tour guide, pointed out that the area had experienced a drought for five years and a bush fire in the year 2009. The year we visited, 2010, the land received a good downpour of rain, and the jungle appeared to have sufficient sustenance for the inhabitants. Our visit took place during the beginning of the spring season in Australia, and the sanctuary was alive and well. I can only imagine the devastating effect the drought and fire had on those fine animals. We were able to see some of the results of this devastation but even more remarkable was the revitalization of the greenery, which in turn meant food for the animals.

Our tour guide pointed out many amazing things to us. One of the things that resonated with me was the ability of the birds and animals to survive whatever came their way. When it became necessary for them to relocate for some unexpected reason, they simply moved. They allowed their instincts to lead them to what they needed to survive. Our guide directed our attention to a family of emus. He explained to us that the emu could be found all across Australia and is the largest bird in the country. They feed on grass, fruit, flowers, bugs, and other insects. While the female is the parent who lay the eggs, once the egg is laid, the male emu actually cares for the unborn chick. He sits on the eggs for eight weeks until they hatch. Once they are born the baby chicks follow the male emu for eighteen months. The mother emu follows the family as well. The father emu is the actual caretaker while the mother has her own interests.

I found it striking that as the father moved about on the land, so went the chicks and the mother. Neither a single chick nor the mother abandoned the father. Although each chick and the mother had their own individual personality, they depended on the father for their directions. When the father walked, the family walked. When the father stopped, the family stopped. The father went to the stream for water, and the family followed. After ten minutes at the stream, the father lifted his head and headed to another section of the park, and his family joined him in this peaceful moment. Despite the many distractions in that park and an awareness of the lurking dangers, this family relied upon the father. It was easy to see that this family had placed their confidence and trust in the father. As long as their eyes were upon the father, they had the assurance that their needs would be met.

Now what lesson did I learn from those birds? If I look at the heavenly Father, keep my eyes on him, move when he moves, just as those emu chicks did, I too will have all that I need. The book of Hebrews encourages Christians to travel with their eyes fixed on Jesus Christ: "fixing our eyes on Jesus, the pioneer and perfecter of faith. For the joy set before him he endured the cross, scorning its shame, and sat down at the right hand of the throne of God" (Hebrews 12:2).

Why Do We Tuck Away, Hide, and Store Things in Barns?

What happened in our lives that caused us to take our eyes off the Father? What are we afraid of? Do we fear that tomorrow there will not be enough bread to eat? Why do we insist on our independence apart from the Father? Do we feel that we can make it on our own without his wisdom? Let us take a quick review:

- We were created in the image of God (Genesis 1:27).
- He put within us a yearning to be like him (Genesis 1:27).
- The only way we can be like God is to spend quality time in his presence (Philippians 2:5).
- We must walk with him, communicate with him, and dine with him (Revelation 3:20).
- We are encouraged to take his yoke upon us and to learn from him (Matthew 11:28).
- Spending time with God should not be a burden to us. It should and must become our delight (Psalm 3:1-3).

The psalmist requested that we "delight ourselves in the Lord and the promise he gives to us is this: we will receive the desires of our heart" (Psalm 37:3-4). These are God's actual desires for us. In 2 Chronicles 7:14, we are told to seek the face of God to gain his favor. These "desires of our hearts" are not personal desires. These are desires from the heart of God that he places within us.

Will Satan do to us as he did to Adam and Eve if given the opportunity? Will he encourage us to take our eyes off of the will of God and aim to become a god in our own right? Will we bite into his idea, believe his lie, and abort God's will? It is most unfortunate that the answer to the above questions is often in the affirmative. Since God has promised to provide for all our needs, let us strive to trust him as do the birds. The next time you have an opportunity to watch bird activity, see if they carry luggage around with them. See if they have storehouses in which to store food supplies. See if they live as though there is no tomorrow. You will notice that they just trust God for all of their needs.

> Therefore I tell you, do not worry about your life, what you will eat or drink; or about your body, what you will wear. Is not life more than food, and the body more than clothes? Look at the birds of the air; they do not sow or reap or store away in barns, and yet your heavenly Father feeds them. Are you not much more valuable than they? Can any one of you by worrying add a single hour to your life? And why do you worry about clothes? See how the flowers of the field grow. They do not labor or spin. Yet I tell you that not even Solomon in all his splendor was dressed like one of these. If that is how God clothes the grass of the field, which is here today and tomorrow is thrown into the fire, will he not much more clothe you—you of little faith? (Matthew 6:25-30)

CHAPTER 8

Do I Need a Survival Pack?

A survival kit is a pack of necessary items that a person needs to have in case of an emergency. Such kits could contain a first-aid pack, water, canned food, a mirror, candle, knife, rope, toilet paper, pen, paper, whistle, flashlight, and batteries. Its purpose is to ensure your survival during an expected or unexpected emergency. It is not intended to be a long-time cure; it is only something to hold you over until you get what you need.

In the year 1999, there was much talk concerning Y2K (the year 2000). Many people were troubled because there were predictions of pending troubles and woes. Someone had the idea that the new millennium would mark the beginning of a world crisis. There would be no electricity; computers would no longer work, which would lead to bigger problems; the water supply would be depleted; and there would be no food. People of every nationality were greatly concerned that the world was in trouble. Someone capitalized on this fear and told people that there was a first-aid kit, a survival pack, that would save them from the problem.

In every town, the talk was about Y2K. The potential computer glitch became such a great concern, seminars and workshops popped up in many churches, businesses, and schools. These workshops created great fear among participants. A large number of pastors saw this as an opportunity to raise some additional funds for their own pockets. From a number of pulpits came messages about the need for a survival pack. The people believed the messages coming from the pulpits because, after all, the pastors represented God, didn't they. Or did they?

I attended one of these gatherings at a prominent church near Chicago. Professionally produced flyers, postcards, billboards, and mailings publicized the event and encouraged people to realize they needed to be prepared for the coming disaster. Radio and television stations advertised the workshop and other Y2K-related seminar locations. Church members helped to promote what I call a demonic lie. Members of my own congregation lived in fear of Y2K. Some of them were long-time members of the church. I could understand weak believers falling for this lie, but when I heard some of the seasoned saints holding animated discussions about Y2K and their fear of the coming New Year, I knew that as a pastor, I needed to address this issue head on. I also knew that I needed to have some authority to support my opposition to the Y2K fear that was sweeping the land into a pile of trash.

Thanks to an invitation from a long-time Christian friend, I made plans to attend the conference. We met in a large and spacious auditorium at her "church house." There was a variety of people—business people, funeral directors, teachers, doctors, pastors—in attendance, which created a standing-room-only situation. I found a seat and observed people as they came into the auditorium. Not knowing what would be said or taught, people looked as though they were coming to hear a "Dear John" letter. Finally, the sounding of the bell was heard, and the people gave their undivided attention to all that took place. There was a period of praise and worship, and then the main event was presented. You could hear a pin drop. The people wanted to know what the experts had to say about our future and how we would collectively be affected by this Y2K problem. The main speaker was introduced by the pastor of the hosting church, which gave credence to the gathering.

Some of the Best Lies Are Told in Church

As I listened to the presentation, it wasn't long before I knew that it was a moneymaking idea that came from the pits of hell. My heart dropped, and as I looked around this church, I remembered that this was not a small thing. If a bomb had hit the building at that hour, a great portion of the land would suffer greatly because of the magnitude of the constituents in attendance that day. What was worse was the fact that so many of them bought into that lie. It was the perfect stage. This was a prominent church, with an influential pastor, and great publicity. It just had to be right. There was no question. Y2K! Y2K! Are you ready for Y2K? They had the people right where they wanted them, eating out of their hands. So much that was said in this setting created a hunger for additional information on this issue. It was at this point that the speaker said, "Our time is up, but to aid you in your survival, you will need to purchase my CDs and books in the rear of the sanctuary so that you will be prepared for Y2K." Some of the items we were encouraged to purchase were cell batteries, canned food, cases of water, freeze-dried foods, and the like. Great emphasis was placed on getting the publications, flyers, and pamphlets about Y2K. The only mention of the Lord by the presenter was that the Lord wanted us to be ready and to make preparations "just in case." As the meeting drew to a close, lines formed at the tables to purchase the survival packs before the benediction was given. As I looked at this deception and misrepresentation of truth, my heart was saddened. I saw people being robbed without a gun while the leaders of this deception saw money and more money. And indeed the big bucks came in at the conclusion of the seminar.

While there was sadness in my heart for the people, I also knew that I had to do something to teach and share the real truth with my congregation about this Y2K issue. My people would not be allowed to perish because they lacked knowledge of the truth of God's Word. I had to fight this deception with the truth found in the Bible. I began to seek the Lord, and he put it in the proper perspective for me. What I heard clearly and out aloud were these words, "Take no thought." I wondered when I should begin teaching my congregation. As the year was ending, we were in our Watch Night service at the church; one of my members showed me that in her purse she had a flashlight that required three D-size batteries. When I asked why she had the flashlight, she replied that there would be no lights after midnight, and she wanted to be able to see in the dark. I knew then that I could not waste any more time. I had to address and spiritually prepare my flock with a series of messages on Y2K. I needed to act immediately.

The Lord Is Our Survival Pack

I searched the scriptures to find passages that assured we did not need to be concerned about the turn of a new century. Many great passages confirmed what I already knew about God's thoughts on and about the future. I went to work on a series of sermons that unpacked bundles of assurances to defeat the notion that God would need help because of a computer chip. In essence, I reminded the people of God what they already knew, but needed reinforced and stirred up in their spirits. The Lord has been, is, and will be all that we will ever need. There is no failure in God. He is sovereign, and this makes him more than enough. When the Lord says to us through his Word, "don't fear," then we should know that this is a reliable assurance. In other words, you can find something else to do with your time other than worry. "Do not be afraid, for I am with you; I will bring your children from the east and gather you from the west" (Isaiah 3:5). In everything, there is what is called the bottom line. In this case, the bottom line is this: the Lord is our survival pack. Without the Lord you will never win, and with the Lord you will never lose. Place your trust in the Lord and in him alone. It is our responsibility to know what the Bible teaches. We must spend time in the Word of God and never neglect good and sound Biblical teaching and preaching. After hearing the Word of God, we must begin to apply it to our daily lives by faith. Proper application will help keep us on the right path and will give us the constant assurance we need to walk in faith and not in doubt. Hebrews 11:6 reminds us of the importance of pleasing God while engaging in active and participatory faith. In light of these things, do we really need an external survival pack that places God on the outside of our lives? This leads me to my next question.

Will God Be in Business Tomorrow?

> I am the Lord thy God and I change not. (Malachi 3:6)

> Jesus Christ is the same yesterday and today and forever. (Hebrews 13:8)

In this world, we are often consumed with wanting to know what someone has said about someone else. "He said, she said" conversations are nothing more than sessions of gossip. The *Oxford Dictionary* defines gossip as "casual or unconstrained conversation or reports about other people, typically involving details that are not confirmed as being true." On any number of occasions people have brought to me juicy information about another person (news that I did not ask for), and I unfortunately listened to the information, made a rash judgment about the person being discussed, and concluded that what was said was true. On too many of those occasions I did not entertain the notion that the person being discussed was innocent until proven guilty. My immaturity encouraged me to take what was said as truth without taking into account who was making the report.

This happens to many people who hear casual bits of talk about others. Our fallen nature desires company, and we soon conclude that since we are not so perfect, neither is that other person; therefore, he is guilty. The only time we challenge a bad report about someone is when we care about the person being discussed. At that point, we might challenge the whisperer with "Are you sure this is true?" Even when told that it is true, we will make our own investigations of the matter before we come to a conclusion. What makes us go the extra mile to verify this new bit of news? Concern and care are the operative words. We do not want to hear anything negative or destructive about someone we love. When you love someone, you care about how they are viewed by others, and you are concerned about their reputation. In our own ways we want to protect and shield our friends and family from predators who seem to find pleasure in bringing others down.

How much do we know about what God has said in the Bible? Our knowledge about God and his Word will assist us whenever a lie is told about God. Satan always seeks to discredit God through lies and gossip. Gossip is a practice God does not consider too kindly, according to Proverbs 6:17: "haughty eyes, a lying tongue, hands that shed innocent blood." Satan has succeeded on many occasions because people simply did not know what God said through his Word or about his nature to oppose what was being said about him. Before the beginning of time, God has been in charge. After God created the heavenly host, nature, the animal world, vegetation, and humankind, he remained the Lord. Throughout history, people have toyed with the notion that they were larger than God and that, if they could get a hearing and a following, they could unseat God and become gods themselves. When you read the annals of history, you will discover that several world leaders have tried everything to disprove the reality of God, but to no avail. They lost the argument due to a lack of evidence. In times past and in this present day, some seek ways to dismiss any notion about the reality of God:

> Since what may be known about God is plain to them, because God has made it plain to them. For since the creation of the world God's invisible qualities—his

> eternal power and divine nature—have been clearly seen, being understood from what has been made, so that people are without excuse. For although they knew God, they neither glorified him as God nor gave thanks to him, but their thinking became futile and their foolish hearts were darkened. Although they claimed to be wise, they became fools and exchanged the glory of the immortal God for images made to look like a mortal human being and birds and animals and reptiles. (Romans 1:19-23)

The atheist movement is composed of those who make a conscious decision not to believe in the reality of God. I personally became acquainted with a few professing atheists whose testimony was "they did not believe in God and therefore, to them, God did not exist.

I heard a story on the radio some time ago about an atheist who stood before a judge to argue his case about the need to have a holiday atheists could call their own. This man argued that all other religions had holidays, such as Christmas, but there was nothing on the calendar for people who do not believe in God. The judge said to this man, "If you are sure that you do not believe in God, there is a holiday set for you: that day is April 1 each year."

> "The fool says in his heart, 'There is no God.' They are corrupt, their deeds are vile; there is no one who does good" (Psalms 14:1).

Satan, in Reality, Is Not in Charge

Now I must confess, there have been times when I wondered if God was still up there. I learned a bit about the power of God, and I learned a great deal about Satan, the "prince of the air": ". . . in which you used to live when you followed the ways of this world and of the ruler of the kingdom of the air, the spirit who is now at work in those who are disobedient" (Ephesians 2:2). I concluded that, just maybe, Satan might be in charge since God allowed him to stir the elements. Thank God that I finally moved from those thoughts, dug back into the Bible, and learned that Satan must obtain God's permission before he can do anything to us.

> And the Lord said to Satan, "Where have you come from?" Satan answered the Lord, "From roaming throughout the earth, going back and forth on it." Then the Lord said to Satan, "Have you considered my servant Job? There is no one on earth like him; he is blameless and upright, a man who fears God and shuns evil. And he still maintains his integrity, though you incited me against him to ruin him without any reason." "Skin for skin!" Satan replied. "A man will give all he has for his own life. But now stretch out your hand and strike his flesh and bones, and he will surely curse you to your face." The Lord said to Satan, "Very well, then, he is in your hands; but you must spare his life." (Job 2:2-6)

In other words, Satan is only in charge of whatever God grants him permission to be in charge of. And since this is true, Satan, in reality, is not in charge of anything. Satan has parameters in which he is allowed to function, and with those parameters come restrictions.

Satan is fully aware of his limitations and therefore is on mission to convince us that since he is the prince of the air, God is limited and helpless until Satan is contained. Think of the many people who agree with Satan that God is helpless. It's no wonder many people both in and out of the church cannot see the light; they've been blinded by this fellow Satan. They have believed a false report about God. Many times I am convinced that people look for God in the wrong places. Now I know that God is everywhere, but the reality is this: God is not in everything and every place. Because of his nature, God just does not have anything to do with certain things. My big case in point: God created Satan, but God is not in Satan. God is not evil. God does no evil, and God does not share in evil. Why? It is not the nature of God to do evil.

> When tempted, no one should say, "God is tempting me." For God cannot be tempted by evil, nor does he tempt anyone; but each person is tempted when they are dragged away by their own evil desire and enticed. Then, after desire has conceived, it gives birth to sin; and sin, when it is full-grown, gives birth to death. (James 1:13-15)

God never has to give in to deception because he is over all that exists. God has nothing to prove to any of us. All of nature speaks of this. "The heavens declare the glory of God," and the earth shows his handiwork, according to Psalm 19:1. Since the world was created by God, there is no other argument. Our vote for or against God does not alter anything about God. God has been in business and will remain in business and has a vast history, according to Psalm 90:1-2.

According to the Bible, God will never change. "I the Lord do not change. So you, the descendants of Jacob, are not destroyed (Malachi 3:6). In life we have a saying, "if it's not broke, don't fix it." Our God needs no fixing, repair, or reminders of his job as God. Note this friendly reminder: he may not respond to you when and how you expect him to do so, but if you move out of the way, God will manifest himself in the most revealing and unusual ways.

We do well to bear in mind that lies are ancient. Lies have been told about God in an effort to turn our hearts and minds away from him. It is my hope, prayer, and effort to encourage people I come in contact with, those who do not have a close relationship with God, to trust him. I also admonish them to connect with a local church where they can learn more about God through a disciplined study of the Bible and in fellowship with other Christians. If we are going to survive this thing called life, with all of its trials and temptations, we, like the psalmist, must aim higher and look beyond what is before us. If you want to make it today and tomorrow, do as did the psalmist in Psalm 121:1-8:

> I lift up my eyes to the mountains—where does my help come from? My help comes from the Lord, the Maker of heaven and earth. He will not let your foot slip—he who watches over you will not slumber; indeed, he who watches over Israel will neither slumber nor sleep. The Lord watches over you—the Lord is your shade at your right hand; the sun will not harm you by day, nor the moon by night. The Lord will keep you from all harm—he will watch over your life; the Lord will watch over your coming and going both now and forevermore.

Inasmuch as you have a choice in whom you will serve, may I recommend the same person Joshua chose to serve?

> Now fear the Lord and serve him with all faithfulness. Throw away the gods your ancestors worshiped beyond the Euphrates River and in Egypt, and serve the Lord. But if serving the Lord seems undesirable to you, then choose for yourselves this day whom you will serve, whether the gods your ancestors served beyond the Euphrates, or the gods of the Amorites, in whose land you are living. But as for me and my household, we will serve the Lord." Then the people answered, "Far be it from us to forsake the Lord to serve other gods! It was the Lord our God himself

who brought us and our parents up out of Egypt, from that land of slavery, and performed those great signs before our eyes. He protected us on our entire journey and among all the nations through which we traveled. (Joshua 24:14-17)

PART THREE

Beyond Tomorrow

CHAPTER 9

Jesus Christ Always the Same

We live in a world that is constantly changing. Many people argue that the world is changing for the better, while others maintain that it is changing for the worst. The truth of the matter is, people have changed. As the days continue, the thoughts, attitudes and actions of people change. While we deny that any of us have changed, the reality is, we all change. I am convinced that we change for several reasons.

First, we mature and grow. As we are fed as infants, toddlers, juniors, and on up to adults and seniors, our bodies stretch, expand, and shrink, until death makes it claim on us. Our clothes and shoe sizes change. It is impossible for us to remain the same.

Second, we grow in wisdom, or at best, we should. Wisdom is the quality of having experience, knowledge, and good judgment. We learn from our experiences, lessons that suggest better ways of accomplishing tasks in the future and with better precision. We vow to ourselves that the next time we tackle a project, we will do it in a certain manner. I have made a great number of mistakes because wisdom was not operating in me, for instance, talking without first thinking something through. Sometimes I have taken an action without first examining the consequences. Most times, I had to buy wisdom because the choices I made proved to be very costly.

Third, our understanding often changes as we age. Where we were once dull in our understanding we now know to do things differently. The things I know now help me determine how to do a better job and with a minimum amount of effort. To understand a thing is to have the correct perspective; without that, your reasoning will be off-center, and you may make a wrong judgment. Wisdom enables a person to apply knowledge to most situations.

As we age and grow, we often declare that we will never change. Again, we make this determination without the benefit of knowing what the future will bring. Everything around us changes, thus leaving us no alternative. As much as we brag about not changing, the truth is, we do. People, nature, and conditions all around us change, some for the better and some get worse.

With all of these changes, we have to explore the issue of reliability. How reliable is anything on the earth? What can we bank on not changing? The answer is nothing. Everything changes—things as well as people. Take automobiles, for example. While the new cars have all the "bells and whistles," they are not as solid as they once were. Electronics and parts that used to be metal and sturdy are now plastic. They cannot take the abuse that the older parts were able to take.

There are new morals and standards for living. Things that were once considered disgraceful have now become the norm for acceptable behavior. At one time, if a female had a child outside of wedlock, it was considered shameful. A couple living together without the benefit of marriage (what people call "sharing space" today) was frowned upon, especially if they were members of a church. Laws have been changed in an effort not to offend people in same-gender relationships. We have even changed how we worship the Living Christ so that people feel comfortable whenever they decide to show up. We were commanded in John 4:24 to worship the Lord in "Spirit and in truth." Instead of obeying this command, we tell people to just "come as you are, and you will not be judged."

People are told that God is not interested in their clothes or lifestyle. To this end, it is hard to determine in some settings whether you are in a house of worship or at a rock concert in the park. Many ministerial circles make allowances so that people will not be offended by the preaching of the Gospel. Some of my contemporaries no longer preach messages that pertain to the cross, the blood of Jesus, or sin and its consequences for fear of losing segments of their membership.

Many relationships have ended because someone was accused of changing. Do you wonder why we are able to see the changes that others have made but deny the ones we have made in our own lives? We must face the fact that everything and everybody will change, and there is no way around this. While there are some things about us that remain constant, such as personality, distinct features and the like, even these will show slight variations as we age.

You Are Going to Change

There are a few things that I have discovered about myself and others around me. The more I try not to change, the more I do change. If you are like me, you become bored doing some things the same way all the time. Sometimes just looking at and making comparisons with how others are living and doing things causes us to make alterations in our lives. If we discover that there is a new way of doing something, we will make that change. If that way doesn't work for us, we will try something else. My point is this: we often change without knowing that we are doing so. If we are going to be better, it only comes as a result of change. This is how we improve. If you do what you have always done in life you will get what you have always received. Even machines, when they break down, require a new part or must be rebooted.

Think about how computers, copiers, telecommunication devices, household appliances, automobiles, aircraft, and the like have been improved over the years. They are doing what they've always done, but now they gain a higher yield. They are more efficient and more complicated. In years past, the average "yard tree mechanic" could just go under the hood and figure out what was wrong with a car. Because of the changes in technology, today you need specialized training to work on cars. This holds true for just about anything else. At one time, your primary doctor did practically everything, perhaps with the assistance of a nurse or two. While there were specialists who treated certain illnesses, your primary doctor was in charge. Now there are restrictions and limitations on everyone and in all professions. Primary physicians often seem to be restricted from doing as they once did and now make referrals to other specialists.

Finally, while we all would like to brag that we do not change and have not changed, nothing could be farther from the truth. We would do well to get used to the fact that we have changed. Everything around us has changed, some for the better and some for the worse. The one fact that we can rest on is this: we have a God, through the person of Jesus Christ, who has not changed, will not change, and cannot change. He cannot improve because there is no need for him to make any improvements. All that he has ever done has been performed with excellence. We change and begin to see things differently because of our growth and development. There is no need for the Lord to change because he is perfect in all his ways. He is a class act without controversy. Jesus Christ is our model of appropriate behavior and what is right. We are seeking to be like him and not make him be like us.

> Be perfect, therefore, as your heavenly Father is perfect. (Matthew 5:48)

> As for God, his way is perfect: The Lord's word is flawless;
> he shields all who take refuge in him. (Psalm 18:30)

My knowledge of an unchanging God gives me solace. I am able to rest in the comfort that my God is consistent in all of his doings. He loved me long before I invited him into my heart to be my savior, while I was yet a sinner. (Romans 5:8) Each time I fell from his mark and did not live up to his expectations, his love for me never changed. When I didn't love myself, he loved me, and it was this love that encouraged me to be patient with myself. Today, I am thankful for a reliable God, in the person of Jesus Christ my Lord. If you need some consistency in your life, I would like to recommend Jesus Christ to you. He will never change.

Finally, who on earth do you know that is without any flaw? Who do you know that is without any sin, shame, or controversy? The Holy Scriptures are correct. According to Romans 3:23, every person is guilty of missing God's mark of perfection. 1 John 1:10 tells us that the person claiming not to have sinned is calling the Lord a liar. We can, and should, collectively thank God for Jesus Christ because he never changes.

Misdirected Faith

> What is faith? "Now faith is being sure of what we hope for and certain of what we do not see." (Hebrews 11: 1)

Faith is a powerful thing, and you should be careful how you direct and where you place your faith. You can use your faith for your advancement or for your failure. Faith, according to the Merriam-Webster's Dictionary is "the confident belief or trust in a person, idea, or thing that is not based on proof." Therefore, faith can be based on proof or evidence and then be projected onto future events.

Everyone has faith, though it may not be not pointed in the same direction. As I mentioned, your faith can work toward your advancement or your demise, because you are the driving force behind it. If faith were an automobile, you would be in the driver's seat with full control of the steering wheel, gas, and the brake pedals. While there are rules to driving on the road, you have to interpret those rules and hope that your interpretation is correct. There are set standards for drivers, but it is up to you to determine how to function with the knowledge and rules you were given. What you do or fail to do while you are behind the wheel will determine whether you are commended or cited for your driving.

Your faith is yours, and it does not belong to anyone else. You are the sole spokesperson for your faith. Your life-long experiences give shape to your faith. Your faith is unique to you and is tailored for your use. Your faith works for you, listens to your voice, will follow your frequency. Your faith is as powerful or as weak as you want it to be. Your faith is in an internal compartment of your own choosing. While others can see evidence of your faith, they do not have access to its power cord or control buttons. Should you share in a faith project with others, there will be a distinct separation between your faith and that of the other person. You do not get to lay blame on God or on others when your faith comes short of your destination.

History and the Bible are filled with people who displayed their faith. We saw what happened with those whose faith was shallow; they didn't go too far.

> That day when evening came, he said to his disciples, "Let us go over to the other side." Leaving the crowd behind, they took him along, just as he was, in the boat. There were also other boats with him. A furious squall came up, and the waves broke over the boat, so that it was nearly swamped. Jesus was in the stern,

> sleeping on a cushion. The disciples woke him and said to him, "Teacher, don't you care if we drown?" He got up, rebuked the wind and said to the waves, "Quiet! Be still!" Then the wind died down and it was completely calm. He said to his disciples, "Why are you so afraid? Do you still have no faith?" They were terrified and asked each other, "Who is this? Even the wind and the waves obey him!" (Mark 4:35-41)

Note, Jesus didn't say to this group, "Let us go and drown." He said, "Let's go to the other side." I have witnessed people both inside and outside my congregation who believed more in their own defeat than in their success and survival. While they could have done better, they didn't, simply because they lacked the faith to advance.

On the other hand, there are those who had great faith, so much that even with faith "the size of a grain of a mustard seed" they were able to do great things. Those who had great faith have always been commended for it. We see examples of these successes in the book of Matthew:

> He answered, "I was sent only to the lost sheep of Israel." The woman came and knelt before him. "Lord, help me!" she said. He replied, "It is not right to take the children's bread and toss it to the dogs." "Yes it is, Lord," she said. "Even the dogs eat the crumbs that fall from their master's table." Then Jesus said to her, "Woman, you have great faith! Your request is granted." And her daughter was healed at that moment. (Matthew 15:24-28)

> So Jesus went with them. He was not far from the house when the centurion sent friends to say to him: "Lord, don't trouble yourself, for I do not deserve to have you come under my roof. That is why I did not

> even consider myself worthy to come to you. But say the word, and my servant will be healed. For I myself am a man under authority, with soldiers under me. I tell this one, 'Go,' and he goes; and that one, 'Come,' and he comes. I say to my servant, 'Do this,' and he does it." When Jesus heard this, he was amazed at him, and turning to the crowd following him, he said, "I tell you, I have not found such great faith even in Israel." (Mark 7:6-9)

John H. Johnson, the founder of *Ebony* magazine, built a multimillion-dollar cosmetics and insurance empire—all from the $500 he borrowed, using his mother's furniture as collateral. Chapter 20 of his book *Succeeding Against the Odds*, is called "Failure Is a Word I Don't Accept":

> For the moment—for a brief moment—I considered the possibility of failure, but the mere thought of the word made my body shake and my heart pound, and I banished it once and for all from my life and vocabulary. I remember firing a young man for using the word failure. "Nothing personal" I said, but I'm too insecure myself to have people around me who believe that failure is a possibility. Failure is a word I don't accept.

When you look at stories like Johnson's, you begin to understand that people achieved success because of their faith, and they exercised it for their advancement. Those who had little to no faith were always disappointed, because they went nowhere and accomplished nothing that was worthy of mention.

Everybody has faith. The real issue is, where is your faith? In whom is your faith placed? Where is your faith directed? Have you taken the time to study where you want your faith to rest? In other words, your faith requires a destination. You must aim your faith in a certain direction. Remember, you are in the driver's seat with your feet on the pedals and your hands on the wheel. You are the one who should know where you are going. You are the one looking out of the window for your destination. There are signs and landmarks along the way to let you know that you are on course. Why? It is because of your faith. Without knowing where you are going, any place will appear to be the place to be. Where is your faith at this moment? What are you attempting to accomplish?

When my father-in-law, Charles Walker, was on his deathbed, he told those of us who were at the hospital, "I'm heading home." One person thought that he was talking about going back to Mississippi and said he was not referring to the right interstate. Charlie said, "I see the signs because Rev. told me what to look for." Charlie was on his way to heaven.

Where is your faith? You are the one who speaks the word of faith, and you are the one who decides where your faith is to go. Your faith knows your voice. If your faith is ever lost, guess how it got lost? If you are feeling a sense of indictment here, please know that this is my intent. No one other than you can speak about your faith. When you go into a department store shopping for a garment, the salesperson can show you all kinds of garments and assure you that you really look good in them. To purchase or not to purchase is your choice alone, no matter how well the garment fits on you. And since you must decide where your faith will rest, your aim must be intentional. If you send faith in a direction without any investigation, the result may not be to your satisfaction. If you fail to do your homework, don't become upset when the teacher issues you a failing grade and don't be upset with other classmates who did their homework and scored well on their exam. It is a fact of life that "you get out of a thing what you put into it."

Did your faith end up in the place you wanted it to be? If so, good, but if your faith is in a strange place, how did it get there? Who put your faith in that location? Again, the salesperson can make suggestions, but it is your call at the end of the day. It is your money. If that garment is not what you want, move on. Why buy something you do not want, only to return it to the store later? Come on, don't you deserve better than that? Do you really have time to run back and forth to a place you don't want to be?

Is Your Faith Properly Aimed?

How many times have you asked yourself, "Why am I at this particular place or point in life, and why am I not any farther along?" How often have you asked, "Why don't things go in the direction I want them to go?" Have you considered the fact that you are the guiding force behind your faith? You alone control where your faith goes. Your faith is like a guided missile. You are at the control tower, and you get to push the buttons. If you do not study the targeted object, your missile may go awry. The energy you project at the wrong object is the energy you propel toward the correct object. Is your faith focused on the wrong areas, things, person, or group? How many times have you made someone a priority in your life even though you were only an option in theirs? Better yet, how many times have you discovered that your faith was misaligned? Let's be clear right here, faith is faith even when it is pointed in the wrong direction. It still remains faith. Is your faith on course?

If your faith is in doubt and focused on what you can't do, is it faith? Yes! It is still faith. This reminds me of headlamps on a car I once owned. I was having difficulty seeing the road at night, and I took the car to an auto-repair shop only to learn that the headlamps were misaligned. The lights were doing what they were designed to do with one exception: they needed to be readjusted. Once the aim was corrected, I was able to see the road. So again, faith will work in any area to which it is aimed.

Is your faith aimed in the direction you are heading, or is it aimed away from your intended pathway? Can you see the road that leads to your destination? Does your faith scratch your itch? The purpose of scratching is to relieve your itch. If you have applied your faith to a situation, and there is no change or improvement, then it may be your faith was misdirected. How many times have you asked God to help you, but your faith was in your expected results rather than in God, who is and should be the object of our faith? Too often we have a hidden agenda and somehow expect God to cooperate with our private desires. This is unfortunate because God always knows what is best for us. If we consult him first and let him determine the results, we will find so much more contentment in our lives. If your faith has been misdirected, there is a solution to this problem, and it is simple. Get the correct perspective and redirect your faith. Focus your faith in the right direction, and do not depend on easy remedies. Understand that there is a process for all things, and your faith will make the connection for you. Do not set yourself up for failure. Trust in the Lord, and allow your faith to honor him, and he will direct your path. "Trust in the Lord with all your heart and lean not on your own understanding; in all your ways submit to him, and he will make your paths straight" (Proverbs 3:5-6).

What do you surround yourself with? Who influences your walk of faith? I am convinced that the failure in some people is so great because they have invested their faith in failure. I have spoken with people who said they wanted to do better than what they were doing. Their weakness was that they did not surround themselves with people who were headed in their direction. They chose to hang with people who were headed in the opposite direction and kept them off their intended paths. These influencers remind me of a bucket of crabs. When a crab tries to climb out of the bucket to free itself, one of the other crabs will bring it back down. I am not sure who said this but it makes my point, "If you want to fly like an eagle, *don't* hang around with turkeys."

"Walk with the wise and become wise, for a companion of fools suffers harm." "(Proverbs 13:20). We must face the harsh reality that some people, places, and things can have a negative impact on our walks of faith. We must be sure about what we are seeking. We must ask, "Do I really want what I am after?" Most times in life, you will find what you look for. Is your faith heading in the right direction, or is it on a collision course with defeat? If you are headed the wrong way and you know it, apply your brakes, regroup, and head in the intended direction. You can do this, but it requires a made-up mind and knowledge of the facts.

CHAPTER 10

Get Some Sleep

He Makes Me Lie Down in Green Pastures

In a number of conversations and in sermons, I have used this line from Psalm 23: "He makes me lie down in green pastures." God makes us to lie down, I've commented, because we do not know how to rest. As I read through the scriptures, I ran across many passages encouraging me to get some rest. There is an eternal rest for the weary: "Then I heard a voice from heaven say, 'Write this: Blessed are the dead who die in the Lord from now on.' 'Yes,' says the Spirit, 'they will rest from their labor, for their deeds will follow them'" (Revelation 14:13). However, there is an earthly rest of which we should take advantage. If you rest properly, you might get some sleep as a bonus. (In your spare time, you may want to read the following passages on rest: Exodus 23:12, Joshua 1:15, Psalm 37:7, and Matthew 11:28-29.)

Rest is vital to good health. This week I was in bed because I had been working nonstop for the last three months. I know the importance of resting and sleeping too well. I preach it, advise it and illustrate it to others. For some apparent reason, I opted not to take my own advice and found myself saying, "He makes me to lie down . . ." I shared this with my friend Rev. James E. Marshall, who said, "While the Bible says green pastures, we often look at it as our having to lie down in misery." We laughed, and I conceded that I was in some misery, but I did get his message. I was down for two days, determining that I needed to treat myself to some wholesome sleep. The two days of restful sleep did me well.

Let me ask you a few searching questions. Do you know how to rest? Do you take the necessary moments to rest and recuperate? How important is sleep to you? Is it a priority to you?

There is a difference between rest and sleep. According to the *New Oxford American Dictionary*, to rest is to "cease work or movement in order to relax, refresh oneself, or recover strength." On the other hand, sleep is a condition of body and mind that typically occurs for several hours every night; the nervous system is relatively inactive, the eyes are closed, the postural muscles are relaxed, and consciousness is practically suspended." How well did you answer my questions above? Did you answer honestly? What were your answers?

Will Your Lack of Sleep Help You Achieve Your Goals?

A number of people deprive themselves of meaningful rest on a regular basis in exchange for the privilege to worry. We know in our hearts that worry can have an adverse effect on our total well-being, and yet we will place upon ourselves a spirit of worry even though it will keep us up past our scheduled bedtimes. If we force ourselves into bed, we will get very little sleep because we will toss and turn until it is time to get up.

How easy it is to tell myself and others, "If you are going to worry, then do not pray; but if you are going to pray, do not worry." This advice is solid with all except one: the person who thinks he can control his feelings of helplessness. He sits up at night, searching for answers, thumbing through his indexes of resources, and wishing for a miracle to free him from the maze he is in. When I refuse to treat myself to rest and sleep, it is difficult for me to function at a high level of competency the following day. Staying up for those extra hours did not add anything of value to my life. It gave me puffy eyes, drained energy, and a great deal of irritability the following morning. The lack of sleep kept me from achieving my goals and clouded my internal sense of direction to the degree that had I walked into my destination, I would have missed it because of fatigue.

"Sleep is a significant health concern and just as important as nutrition, exercise and stress management," writes Timi Gustafson, a clinical dietitian, health counselor and author:

> While we sleep at night, we heal and recuperate from the wear and tear of our day. Unfortunately, more and more people find it necessary to cut back on their sleep. The consequences for their health and quality of life can be devastating. In fact, sleep deprivation has become such a widespread phenomenon, that some states have enacted legislation that defines "fatigued driving" in similar terms to drunk driving. Lack of sleep is not only a potential health hazard; it affects the safety of everyone on the road and at the work place.
>
> Clinical studies have shown that sleep deprivation can be a contrbuting factor to a number of lifestyle-related illnesses—among them obesity, diabetes, hypertension and heart disease. Patients with persistent sleep deficits have routinely shown alterations in their metabolism, inhibiting their ability to manage glucose levels by making their cells increasingly insulin resistant.

Sleeplessness can lead to imbalances in the release of stress hormones, such as cortisol. Potential consequences are weakening of the immune system, risk of a variety of chronic illnesses as well as psychological effects, such as memory loss, mood swings and depression. Sleep deprivation may also have a significant impact on one's life expectancy.

On the upside, there is compelling evidence that a healthy sleep routine can contribute greatly to one's physical and mental well-being as well as the quality of life in general. Getting sufficient sleep ranks among the best defense mechanisms we have to stay healthy and handle our stress. We function and perform at our best when we are well-rested. We are better colleagues, parents, companions and lovers when we are relaxed and at ease. We face challenges with more energy and resolve and keep negative or destructive emotions at bay. We are less prone to reach for drugs or alcohol to get high or numb ourselves when the going gets tough. In a word, with enough rest, we are more likely to stay healthy and well all around.

To help me write this chapter, I wanted to include others, in an effort to glean what I could about this issue of rest and sleep and our need to get as much of it as possible. What is the reality? I asked a few questions to twenty people, some I knew and a few I didn't, between ages twelve and ninety—and experiences in life. I paid them for permission to use their names and comments in my book.

<u>Why Is It Important to Get Some Sleep?</u>

Ages 12-18

1. Kyra: "Because getting rest will help you and you need rest in order to succeed in life."
2. LaShaundra: "So that you will have energy for the rest of your day. You should also get sleep so that you will focus in school or at work."
3. Issia: "Sleep helps you to grow and you need growth."

Ages 19-27

1. Charles: "So you won't be restless."
2. Alisha: "So that you can be attentive and focused."
3. LaToya: "To interact well with others."

Ages 28-40

1. Janell: "To be more alert and have more energy. It also changes your mood (to a better one)."
2. Perry: "To keep the body healthy, especially the mind."
3. Jamie: "For health, to be well rested, and so my coworkers don't kill me."

Ages 41-65

1. Kevin: "I don't feel as sharp mentally, or energetic physically, when I don't get a good night's sleep. It's healthy."
2. Patricia "It is important for me to get six hours of sleep so that I can function and be at my best."
3. Laura: "To feel well and not crabby. To function at my best."
4. Carrie: "Sleep heals, repairs, and regenerates the body. Sleep is essential for our health and well-being. This is how God designed the body to function."
5. Eugene: "My body feels very tired without it."
6. Jill: "Sleep is essential to good health, and it refreshes the mind and body."
7. Kimberly: "Because it make me feel energized."
8. Betty Lina: "Need to rest, need to relax my mind, and [need my] physical body to be healthy. Gives the body cells an opportunity [to rid] themselves of waste and [repair] themselves."

Ages 67-90

1. Christine: "Since sleep is a time when the body is restored, a time of complete rest, peace, and a natural unconsciousness, it is necessary for me to experience a good night's sleep in order for my body to be ready to perform its normal duties daily."
2. James: "Sleep energizes my body. It enables me to reestablish myself from a draining day. Sleep helps to restore my brain activity so I can think better, process

my thoughts, and engage in meaningful conversation. As a problem-solver, [I find that] sometimes a ten—to fifteen-minute power nap will do me a world of good. I don't need hours on end of sleep, I need restful sleep, which could be as short as thirty minutes or as long as an hour. Without restful sleep, I would not be able to function properly."

3. Gloria: "So that I will function more effectively during the hours that I am awake. Additionally, it is important as well for maintaining good health."
4. Mary: "Because my body needs to be energized and relaxed, so that I can be alert and focused for the work and cares of the next day."

What Prevents You from Sleeping?

Ages 12-18

1. Kara: "Listening to music, writing, walking, and running."
2. Issia: "Brothers, sisters, and noise."
3. LaShaundra: "Staying up studying. I sometimes stay up [using] Facebook or Twitter."

Ages 19-27

1. Charles: "Nothing."
2. Alisha: "Stress and worries."
3. LaToya: "Excitement, confusion, and when I am discouraged."

Ages 28-40

1. Janell: "STRESS!!!"
2. Perry: "[When my] mind is wandering."
3. Jamie: "Time worrying."

Ages 41-65

1. Kevin: "Not much, but sometimes worries, difficult situations, and the like will cause sleeplessness."

2. Patricia: "When I think about bills and I cannot pay on time or health issues."
3. Laura: "Stress, thinking about different situations, my boys."
4. Carrie: "I fall asleep easily. I keep life's stresses in check as best as I can, because staying awake and worrying doesn't solve anything. I pray and talk to God, which gives me peace and a sound mind. I do, however, like to wait up if my boys are out late."
5. Eugene: "The pressures of everyday life."
6. Jill: "Paperwork, work, worrying, and a love for reading. I can't find time during the day so I read very late at night."
7. Kimberly: "Stress."
8. Betty: "[Because I am] worried, [have] lots of work pending, [am] presenting end-of-year accounting report, and time just keeps running."

Ages 67-90

1. Christine: "When I am frustrated or worried about family problems, I find myself unable to fall asleep. My way of relaxing is by repeating Psalm 23. After a period of time, I am usually fast asleep."
2. James: "I've had years of sleepless nights. Studying and cramming for tests, stress on the job. Worry was also the culprit . . . due to bills, ill-health, anxiety, uneasiness, and family chaos . . . If I have a lot on my mind, I become mentally fatigued; that makes me irritable and I'm unable to sleep. There was a time I was tested for sleep apnea. That turned out negative.
3. Gloria: "Reading past bedtime, watching television, mentally planning for the next day's activity, loud music, and/or television and radio; snoring."
4. Mary: "Being overtired, illness, concerns and apprehension will keep me from sleeping."

How Does the Lack of Sleep Affect You?

Ages 12-18

1. Kara: "I [may] believe that if I don't get enough rest, I will fall asleep [the next day] and [won't] concentrate."
2. Issia: "It affects me because I have an attitude problem when I can't sleep."
3. LaShaundra: "It becomes hard to wake up for my eight o'clock classes, and I sometimes sleep the whole day away."

Ages 19-27

1. Charles: "A whole lot."
2. Alisha: "Lack of sleep can make you aggravated and you become a loose cannon all over the place"
3. LaToya: "Headaches and pains in my body."

Ages 28-40

1. Janell: "Not in a good mood, crabby, very forgetful. I sometimes can't comprehend. I ask you the same question over and over."
2. Perry: "Body sluggish and tired."
3. Jamie: "I'm crabby! Very tired all day."

Ages 41-65

1. Kevin: "Since it saps my energy and focus, I tend to have a more difficult day when I'm short on sleep."
2. Patricia: "A lack of sleep makes me move at a slow pace, and I become irritable and quiet."
3. Laura: "I don't feel well, get impatient, crabby and become overwhelmed."
4. Carrie: "If I don't get enough sleep or rest, my body will feel the stress. The body suffers, and I cannot properly function if it is not given the rest that's needed to renew itself."
5. Eugene: "I'm very irritable and cranky all day."

6. Jill: "Lack of sleep causes alterations in my mood, irritability, and grogginess."
7. Kimberly: "I am somewhat sluggish throughout the day."
8. Betty: "Tiredness, no concentration, not productive for the next day."

Ages 67-90

1. Christine: "The lack of sleep causes me to be irritable, feel weak and faithless, [and] experience fear and places a feeling of insecurity in my spirit."
2. James: "I'm unable to think properly, my concentration is less than what it should be, my system seems to slow down, and my mood changes. I have found myself dozing at the wheel while driving, but not fall asleep while talking on the phone."
3. Gloria: "I am agitated, tired, cannot function at 100 percent, irritable, unkind."
4. Mary: "The lack of sleep hampers my mobility, time management, and focus."

As these responses indicate, sleep and proper rest are essential to good health. The lack of sleep and rest will result in negative feelings and behaviors. A member of our congregation, Patricia A. Cooper, in addition to being a devoted Christian woman, is a licensed and registered dietitian. She told me:

> It is important to develop good sleep habits during life. Most adults need eight hours of sleep, and children may need ten to twelve hours of sleep. Many people don't realize that getting an insufficient amount of sleep can affect their mood, attitude, and energy level. Also, research has shown that judgment and reaction times to various situations can be affected by insufficient sleep. The amount of sleep that a person needs will increase if they have been sleep deprived, and the body will eventually require

> the sleep and rest that it needs. Taking naps can also play an important role in supplying a person's needed rest. Adequate sleep is vital for refreshing and renewing our bodies and minds and improving our health.

Your computer, iPad, laptop, work station, job, sports, school, friendships, and family are not replacements for rest. People often misquote the passage from scripture and say, "There's no rest for the weary." Isaiah 57:20-21 says, "There is no rest for the wicked." If Jesus found it necessary to get some rest and sleep (see Mark 6:31), what do you think about us? Are you staying up past your bedtime? I humbly advise you to go to bed!

CHAPTER 11

Get Back into the Word of God

> Do not merely listen to the word, and so deceive yourselves. Do what it says.
>
> (James 1:22)

One of the greatest needs we have as people of faith is to return to the place where we were first empowered, where there was vision and insight, to a place where we were able to find comfort and security. This special place is found in the Word of God. It is where we are able to stand against the tricks of Satan, according to Ephesians 6:10. It is in the Word of God where we hear God speak to us in a language that we understand. After all, God's Word "is a lamp for my feet, a light on my path" (Psalm 119:105).

I must confess that my very first memory of the Word of God was in my home, taught by my mother, Nellye Mae Winfrey. The second place the Word of God was taught to me was in the Sunday School at the Mt. Olive Missionary Baptist Church in Altgeld Gardens in Chicago. (Although there was powerful, anointed preaching and teaching at the Calvary Bible Church on the city's west side, I do not remember much about it because I was very young.) In addition, during the summer, Missionary Stephens did a Bible camp for the young people, and this had a great impact on me. I learned from this missionary how I could apply the Word of God to my life.

My mother taught us the Bible, gave us Bible drills, taught us to memorize the books in the given order, and reminded us that "cleanliness was next to godliness." She made sure we both knew and did what the Bible taught. She was convinced that the Word of God was not just a book to have in church for worship. She linked the Bible to everyday life and said that we would one day have to give an account to God for everything we did. Much of what my mother taught us was based upon her knowledge of the Lord. She had experiences with a few denominations and with different disciplines and doctrines. We landed at the Baptist level, and this is where I am today. And believe it or not, while my mom was once my Bible teacher, I now have the privilege of teaching her the Word of God. It is a great honor and blessing that she is still here and is an active member of our congregation.

Now there are a lot of denominations and religions in the world. I am not seeking to persuade you to change where you are worshipping. What I am advocating is the need to return to the Word of God. Denominations are important because they ensure that there is something for everybody. Some people need one type of conditioning, and some need a different type. Some appreciate a quiet and refined worship experience, some want a more upscale experience, and some want to swing and hang from the light fixtures. The "however" goes right here: at the end of the day, only the Word of God and whether you obey it or not is what matters. The Word of God is right. The Bible shares with us the past, present, and future events. In the Word of God, I have been able to find hope, peace during many storms in life, joy in the midst of sorrow, assurance, comfort during troubling situations, and light in the midst of darkness, and above all, I have been able to find an anchor for my soul. Because of the Word of God, I am able to live an abundant life through Jesus Christ, my Lord. It was Jesus who said, "For truly I tell you, until heaven and earth disappear, not the smallest letter, not the least stroke of a pen, will by any means disappear from the Law until everything is accomplished" (Matthew 5:18). In layman's terms, God's word is reliable and will never be diminished.

There are those who teach, "All roads lead to God, and any church is as good as the next." In *All Roads Lead to One God,* Stacey Chillemi says;

> I grew up in a house of many religions. My father came from Greece raised in a Greek Orthodox background. Even though my father came from a religious home he never posed himself as an overly religious man. When he came to the US and married my mother he didn't encourage the idea of raising a family with the orthodox background.
>
> The Greek Orthodox churches in US speak 50/50. Half the mass would be in Greek and half in American. My father wasn't very religious and he never bothered to teach me Greek so going to a Greek orthodox church wasn't very comfortable especially when you had no idea what they were talking about most of the time.
>
> My mother came from a Jewish background, but never followed the Jewish religion. Her parents weren't religious at all. My mother would take me church hopping all the time as a kid. Lutheran, Baptist—you name [it,] we were there! And most of my friends were Catholic. I still remember sleeping over my friend Marie's house on a Saturday night. The next morning her father would take us to church for morning mass. We would fall asleep on each other's shoulders from staying up too late the night before. Her father would sit in back of us punching us in the shoulders to stay awake.

> No matter what church I went to the message was still the same. To live life loving yourself, loving and caring for the people around you and to make choices in life that would make Christ proud. We can't be perfect. No one is, but the secret is to do your best. Failure only exists in the ones who choose to give up. The ones who try never fail. No matter what the outcome. Years later, I married a faithful devoted Catholic and now we raise our children Catholic. I don't want them to grow up with a confused idea of religion like I had growing up.
>
> But if you ask me I enjoyed the Baptist church the best, because everything was quoted straight from the bible and when the pastor spoke he spoke with a love for Christ that I never have seen since then. I still remember him. What a sweet and caring man. He looked like the grandpa everyone wanted. He was always there for me in many times of confusion and in the obstacles intervened in my life. He was there to help.
>
> I now go to church with my husband, and we are raising our children Catholic, but I haven't seen a pastor or priest talk about Christ with such compassion since then. In my opinion, all roads lead to one God. There isn't any wrong or right religion. If it works for you and it gives you the strength, wisdom and serenity to live in happiness and the will to do good, then so be it.

I do not believe all roads lead to God; some of those roads are heading in the wrong direction. When asked by others which church they should attend, I recommend a church where the Bible is believed and practiced. It is important to be in a place where the Gospel of the Lord Jesus is being taught and preached as well as lived and demonstrated by the leaders in that particular congregation. I am not saying that your house of worship will be spotless and sin free; what I am saying is there must be models of Christ-like behavior, and this begins with the leadership of that congregation. To preach the Word and not live it is a contradiction of what the Bible teaches and is a poor example of a professing Christian.

If you were once involved in reading, studying, and obeying the Bible and have left those good traits, I beg you to return to the Word of God. Apparently something or someone convinced you that this was the right thing to do, and you did it then, and now you are on the sidelines. What caused you to leave the Word of God, which is just as powerful now as it has ever been? Did you run into a great disappointment and begin to believe that God was no longer in charge of this universe? If so, I encourage you to believe me on this matter because God is still in control. No matter how much Satan wags his tongue, hurls his insults toward you, and tells his lies about God, the Word of God remains true. I want to urge you with all of my might to return to God's Word.

If you are too weak to believe, find someone who can represent the best of God and mentor you back to God. Being in a good and fruitful Bible community of believers will guide you back into the loving and capable hands of the Lord. Remember the father of the prodigal sons; his arms were outstretched, saying in essence, "Come on home my child." Home is where the heart is. Are you on the outside looking in? If so, come on in. Have you wandered far from the peaceful shores of the rest that are reserved for the righteous? If so, come on home. It is really that simple. Perhaps you wandered (as wayward sheep) away from the fold and found yourself in a hole of sin, shame, and degradation, wrestling over the guilt of your move. Come on back to God. Listen to what God says: "'Come now, let us settle the matter,'" says the Lord. 'Though your sins are like scarlet, they shall be as white as snow; though they are red as crimson, they shall be like wool. If you are willing and obedient, you will eat the good things of the land; but if you resist and rebel, you will be devoured by the sword.' For the mouth of the Lord has spoken" (Isaiah 1:18-20).

As a believer, it is not enough for you to just attend a one—to two-hour church service at your convenience. You should be involved in a disciplined Bible study, preferably with your pastor or someone the pastor designates to teach the Bible class. In other words, a person can attend the church service and not be a student of the Bible. If this is you, and you have been missing in action, why not consider returning to Bible class/study so that your soul will prosper. Remember the words of Jesus Christ as he spoke to Satan: "Man shall not live by bread alone, but by every word that proceeds from the mouth of God . . ." If you desire the real power that comes from heaven above, get back into the Word of God. Someone said that B-I-B-L-E spelled out is the acronym for "Basic Instructions Before Leaving Earth." The bottom line is, you do not have to live outside of the comfort of God's house. Come on home or, as some have said, "Get back in the saddle."

<u>A Word from Our Sponsor</u>

> Jesus said, "Come to me, all you who are weary and burdened, and I will give you rest." (Matthew 11:28)

Jesus Christ is the author and finisher of our faith. In him dwells the fullness of the Godhead. He is the Word that was with God in eternity past, because he is God. His Word is the only word that will ever count for all eternity. When he speaks, all ears should listen because what he has to say to us is the only thing worth retaining. There is something that is very soothing about how the Lord speaks to us. When Jesus speaks to us, he also gives us the assurance that we can do what he is commanding or urging us to do. For example, when he says "Come unto me, and I will give you rest," there is no need to fret or fear, because it really is okay for us to go. If he invites us to come, he will also supply our needs. The thing I appreciate about the call of Jesus is his calls are never harsh or intimidating.

C. Austin Miles wrote this hymn in 1912:

> I come to the garden alone, while the dew is still on the roses. And the voice I hear, falling on my ear, the Son of God discloses.
>
> He speaks and the sound of his voice is so sweet, the birds hush their singing. And the melodies that he gave to me, within my heart is ringing.
>
> I'd stay in the garden with him, tho the night around me be falling. But he bids me go, thru the voice of woe, his voice to me is calling.
>
> And he walks with, and he talks with me, and he tells me I am his own. And the joy we share, as we tarry there, none other has ever known."

Just think, we have a heavenly sponsor who communicates to us on a regular basis and as we permit him to do so. When you hear the clear voice of Jesus, pay careful attention and do exactly what he tells you to do.

No matter where you are in life, Jesus can and will speak to you, if you only listen. Sometimes I think we miss hearing the voice of Jesus because we are waiting to be yelled at. Perhaps you are surrounded by a group of people who do not care for you. Some of them might have written you off and have abandoned you, which can cause you to worry about what you have done wrong. Maybe you are in declining health or in the twilight years of your life.

Please find comfort in the words of our sponsor when he says, "I will never leave you nor forsake you." When we trust in the Lord, he faithfully gives us direction for our journey. If we can only remember to walk by faith and not by the things our eyes can see, we will do so much better. If you want to do well in this life of yours, remember how Mary, the mother of Jesus, admonished his disciples: "Do whatever he tells you to do." These instructions serve as a reminder that all situations in life do not have to always be complicated. People often intentionally complicate their own lives.

Allow me to conclude by saying to you, be good to yourself; avoid thoughts, actions, attitudes, situations, and people that add unnecessary drama to your life that you do not need. Elevate your mind, determine to raise your aim, think thoughts that will promote life, and by all means pay heed to the strong admonition our Lord gave before you and I were ever born and know that he was very clear when he said, "Take no thought." This is not to say do not think at all; rather it is a strong encouragement for us to simply think *differently* about everything that confronts us.

If you are ready to live the abundant life that our Lord has provided for us by virtue of his life, death on Calvary, burial, resurrection, ascension, and his imminent return, then turn your eyes upon the Savior, in the person of Jesus Christ, and choose life rather than death. If you are going to think at all, think about things that are true, pure, right, holy, friendly, and proper. Don't ever stop thinking about what is truly worthwhile and worthy of praise.

Conclusion

It is my sincere prayer that this simple approach to taking another look at and thinking anew about how you should handle consuming thoughts and actions will bless you with new insights and tools for surviving the entrapments that worry can cause. Resolve to live and not merely to exist. Do not worry about tomorrow, because tomorrow will worry about itself. Do not borrow any trouble from anything or from any person. Refuse and reject anything that competes with the peace that only God can give you. Reject the thought that God does not love you and that this is the reason for your suffering and pain.

Please remember that every life will encounter some trouble, whether or not you consider the work of the enemy of your soul, whose purpose it is to steal, kill, and destroy. Wishful thinking will never relieve you of your stress and worries. You must make an intentional effort to get rid of your worries by having faith in God.

Remember, Jesus said that he came that we might have life with all its benefits; therefore, *take no thought*.

Thank you for reading this book and I pray that you will begin to think differently by taking no thought for your life. Place your full trust in the Lord by seeking his kingdom and his righteousness. God bless you.

TAKE NO THOUGHT
References by Chapters

CHAPTER 1

1. Wiersbe, Warren W. (1979) *"The Strategies of Satan"* Carol Stream, IL Tyndale House, pages 16, 19, 25

CHAPTER 2

1. Marzano, Lisa (1999) *"Too Busy to Obey?"* Colorado Springs, CO, NAV Press, May/June 1999 of Discipleship Journal
2. Hayes, Charles G. (1963) *"No Place, No Where"* Chicago, IL http://youtube/ Y1reIAqJMk
3. Palmer, Horatio R. (1868) *"Yield Not to Temptation"* http://cyberhymnal.org/htm/y/i/yieldnot.htm
4. Pickett, Ludie, (1897) *"Never Alone"* http://cyberhymnal.org/htm/n/e/neveralo.htm

CHAPTER 3

1. Clearing the Jungle http://www.pbs.org/wgbh/americanexperience/features/general-article/jonestown-guyana/

CHAPTER 4

1. Stead, Louisa M. R. (1882) *"Tis So Sweet to Trust in Jesus"* *http://cyberhymnal.org/htm/t/i/tissweet.htm*
2. Hall, Elvina M (1865) *"Jesus Paid it All"* *http://www.hymntime.com/tch/htm/j/p/a/jpaidall.htm*

CHAPTER 5

1. Robbins, Dale A. *http://www.victorious.org/catalog.htm* "The New Age Movement: What Christians Should Know"
2. Hoffman, Elisha A. (1887) http://www.hymnary.org/text/what_a_fellowship_what_a_joy_divine

CHAPTER 6

1. Ten Ways to Stay Young http://www.articlesbase.com/anti-aging-articles/10-ways-to-stay-young-secret-to-staying-young-4199478.html#ixzz1UR3PX2L7

CHAPTER 7

1. *Global Hunger* http://www.bread.org/hunger/global/ Butler, Samuel, BrainyQuote.com, Xplore Inc, 2013. http://www.brainyquote.com/quotes/quotes/s/samuelbutl122806.html, accessed June 6, 2013. Read more at http://www.brainyquote.com/citation/quotes/quotes/s/samuelbutl122806.html#JDFo8UfwQlg2EuiC.99

CHAPTER 10

1. Gustafson, Timi This is an excerpt from an article written by Timi Gustafson R.D., first published at Food and Health with Timi Gustafson R.D. a health and lifestyle blog *"Week 6: The Importance of Sleep For Your Health"* http://www.timigustafson.com

CHAPTER 11

1. Chillemi, Stacey *"All Road Lead to One God"* *http://www.authorsden.com/visit/viewArticle.asp?id=27457*
2. Miles, Austin C. (1912) *"In the Garden"* http://www.hymnlyrics.org/mostpopularhymns/inthegarden.php

CPSIA information can be obtained at www.ICGtesting.com
Printed in the USA
LVOW06s2002210713

343851LV00001B/2/P

9 781475 995398